D0479416

Thinking Class

Related Titles from South End Press

Thinking Class

Sketches from a Cultural Worker

by

Joanna Kadi

South End Press — Boston, MA

Library of Congress Cataloging-in-Publication Data
Kadi, Joanna.
Thinking class: sketches from a cultural worker/ by Joanna Kadi.
    p.   cm.
Includes bibliographical references and index.
ISBN 0-89608-548-1 (cloth: alk. paper). — ISBN 0-89608-547-3 (pbk.: alk. paper)
1. Kadi, Joanna. 2. Working class lesbians—United States—Biography. 3.
Minority women—United States—Biography. 4. Arab Americans—Biography.
5. Adult child abuse victims—United States—Biography. I. Title.
  HQ75.4.K3A3 1996
  306.76'63'092—dc21   96-46462
                                        CIP

 745-C

South End Press, 7 Brookline Street, Cambridge, MA 02139
www.southendpress.org

06 05 04 03 02   3 4 5 6 7

For Jan

Without you,
this wouldn't be possible.

Table of Contents

Acknowledgments

First and foremost, I want to thank my lover, Jan Binder. She consistently provided editing help, emotional support, humor, validation, and ideas. She also pushed me to think more deeply about the issues I explore in this book.

I'm very grateful for the help I received from Asha Mehrling, whose editing skills vastly improved my manuscript. Thanks, Asha, and thanks to the South End collective for their commitment to quality writing and social change.

Thank you to Jimmy Bishara, Elizabeth Clare, Jim Fairhart, Sally Ann Farrar, Marjorie Huebner, Judith Katz, Cynthia Lane, Lisa Suhair Majaj, Beni Matias, Charlotte and Joseph Michael, Nasreen (Naseer) Mohammed, Jeff Nygaard, Juliana Pegues, Elissa Raffa, Susan Raffo, Eleanor Savage, Linda Simon, Linda Suzuki, and Beth Zemsky. Big hugs to Eleanor, Jan, Juliana, Naseer and Susan—you'all know what for. Let's not let Jose get lonely.

The writing/cultural work of Dorothy Allison, Leslie Feinberg, Audre Lorde, and Edward Said has inspired me over the years. I want to acknowledge the impact they've had on me, and express my gratitude for their work.

A special thanks to Dr. Katie Geneva Cannon, writer, educator, thinker. Studying with Dr. Cannon for two years developed my thinking around social issues—particularly around class—profoundly.

Preface

I didn't write this book alone. Don't imagine a lone rugged individual fixedly concentrating in her study with the door firmly closed against any intruders—human, feline, or canine. For one thing, I don't have a study with a door. We can't afford a bigger apartment, although the dogs and cats have been demanding one for some time. For another, I'm blessed with an incredible community, which provided day-to-day support, editing help, and idea clarification. In the fine working-class tradition of barn raisings and quilting bees, a group effort marks these pages.

Without discounting the incredible amount of work I did, I'm focussing here on communal aspects of working-class experience reflected in my life and writing. I grew up in an extended family and a small neighborhood where people frequently asked for help and always got it. Broken-down cars, leaky taps, or sick kids didn't mean a phone call to a costly expert. We knocked on the door of the neighbor who had what we needed.

We indulged in no myths about triumphant figures riding off into the sunset, pursuing fame and fortune at corporate headquarters. We had no horses. If monthly bills got paid, things were good. Occasionally we showed up at corporate headquarters, but we never got inside; we walked in circles near the front door, holding picket signs and megaphones. Most importantly, we weren't raised to believe we could do it alone, and I'd never trade this dependence on and interaction with community for any fictitious rugged individualism.

I use words like "myth" and "fictitious" deliberately, to pinpoint the lie behind the writer as lone figure. My preference for community isn't an individual quirk or choice; no one creates a book on her or his own, although some authors like to give that impression. These are usually privileged people with that unattractive habit of not noticing the peons around them who type their squiggles, clarify their statements, cook supper every night, and provide a pleasant, stress-free work environment.

Every essay in this book has been read by several people, and I've incorporated most of their suggestions. Artwork from my lover, Jan, and from my grandmother grace the cover and pages of the manuscript. The title came from the South End collective. *Thinking Class* perfectly pulls together the notion of thinking about class, and the fact that thoughtful, intellectual activity emerges from the working class, and alludes to the book as a class or forum on thinking.

The word "sketch" appears in the subtitle thanks to Jan. A sketch implies unfinished ideas, works in progress. My thinking about class, and other social issues discussed here, will continue to deepen and change. This book doesn't represent the be-all and end-all of my analysis; referring to sketches leaves room for pushing on with this work.

Further, a sketch gets away from the notion that one lone person can access The Truth. We make sense of tough political issues of race, class, gender, ability, sex, and imperialism when we hear from many different voices and analyze them critically. Social analysis emerges from communities; no one person can do it all or perceive it all.

A faulty premise of western thought (one of many) has to do with the search for One Objective Final Truth. Truth can't be static or finished or complete; it's multi-layered, changing, ever-deepening, originating from many sources. I'm not falling into the worst of liberal relativism by articulating these points; I'm urging us to push on with our search for meaning and explanation, to offer the truth as we perceive it, to thoughtfully reflect within our communities without making universal claims and arrogant assumptions.

As a working-class Arab halfbreed queer girl, I am directly impacted by class, race, imperialism, gender, and sexuality. My writing is steeped in the specifics and particularities of my life experiences; hopefully, my stories and analyses also convey meaning for others.

A great deal of labor went into this book, and the cover reflects that. Drafts, incomplete drawings, crumpled balls of paper, and pencil sketches connect with the sketch concept. The cover also illustrates the working-class ability to create beauty with what we find around us, including everyday objects and accessible materials. Expensive tools, professional plans, and costly training aren't necessary.

This preface provides a clear example of what I mean by communal support for and involvement in my work. I severely burned my right hand the day before I had to begin writing it. Freaked out by the accident, I feared I wouldn't remember Jan's ideas about why the word "sketch" in the subtitle fit so well with the rest of the book. So she jotted down notes, and those ideas set the framework for this preface. My wonderful friends—Nasreen, Juliana, Cynthia, Susan, and Eleanor—came through with emotional support, miso soup, doggy care, and jokes. Jan typed my left-handed scrawls into the computer, frequently kissed my right hand, and assured me everything would come out fine.

And so, in the spirit of community, resistance, and hope, I invite you to jump in and read.

Writing as Resistance, Writing as Love

whose world?

Hunched over on a small chair in the library's corner, I'm invisible in my physical surroundings and on the pages I'm devouring. It's my usual Saturday morning extravaganza—read until nauseated, stagger back to the house with an armful of books, snatch every free moment during the week, dive in.

Books shone brightly on the desolate landscape of my childhood, in ways both profound and basic. They provided fantasy, escape, a reality in stark contrast to the one around me. I especially loved reading about children with happy home lives and positive experiences with a friendly, bustling outside world. But equally profoundly, books, and the children who inhabited their pages, betrayed me by ignoring my world. Where was I? Where were workers? Arabs? Rarely to be found. And if found, never a good word. Stupid janitors who couldn't think, idiotic truck drivers who couldn't write, dirty Arabs who couldn't be trusted.

And still I read, still I coveted shelves full of books, still no one could offer a better present than a book. Still I carried a deeply buried and mostly jumbled desire to carve my own niche in this world. Yet I couldn't imagine anything other than renewing my library card year after year, reading someone else's stories—entering this world of words and books on someone else's terms.

Similar feelings plague me today, after working as a writer for several years. Is there a place for me? Claiming writer status remains so difficult I can barely say the words. If I manage to, I fight the impulse to cover my mouth with my hand, the exact same motion made by toothless family members. Fear and shame prompt their gestures, and my impulse. Who ever heard of someone from a general motors city, destined for secretarial work (if a great deal of luck came her way), thinking, *saying*, she can write books? Who ever heard of a working-class Lebanese writer?

daring tongue maneuvers

I pace back and forth in the living room of the ugly apartment my lover and I rent. We pay too much money for it and the creepy landlord never fixes things when they break. I'm getting small shocks from the shag rug and the radio's turned up. Every day I change my mind. I'll never turn on the news because the American media has taken lies and distortions to new levels in this particular imperialist venture taking place in the Persian Gulf. No. I'll keep the radio on all the time because it might alleviate my feeling of utter helplessness a tiny bit.

This day, tuned into public radio, I hear someone introduce Edward Said very distinctly: "Edward Said is an Arab-American intellectual." This astonishes me. Edward Said has ten minutes to talk about American imperialism and anti-Arab racism? Miracle of miracles. But then the full impact hits and I don't hear anything Said says. Someone, a talk show host on national radio no less, used "Arab" and "intellectual" in the same sentence. And not as part of a comedy routine. The words catch in my chest and something tears wide open. Arab-American intellectual. Can it be possible? Do these words fit together? Can the combination work?

I've always understood the power of words. Certain words can be crunched together into a hard ball and flung with lightning speed. They can knock you off your feet and leave you gasping for breath. It happened to me with the word Arab. People enjoyed hurling word combinations at me—Arab whore, greasy Arab, crazy Arab—and bowling me over, day after day. I never believed anyone who said, "Sticks and stones can break my bones but names can never hurt me." Names did hurt me.

Then, a turning point, a revelation. Words hurt; they also heal. Words jostle my insides, wake me up, jump-start my brain. Someone can place "Arab" side by side with "intellectual" and say it over the radio and the earth moves. And if I can keep my understanding of the power of words front and center while I devise my own wild mixtures, maybe I can open up worlds for people like me, maybe I can offer my writing for healing and resistance.

the importance of silence

The ropes around my ankles and wrists cut into my skin, but the tightest gag cuts across my mouth and tears into the corners. Before tying me up, my father tells me, "You're so bad. You're so bad." Over and over. After he stalks out of the room and slams the door, I try to figure out what I did. I wrack my brain, but nothing comes to mind. Time crawls by. Has one hour passed, or five, or ten? Finally, my father decides—relying on some internal method I can never discern—he should undo the knots. I crawl into bed and hold myself every bit as tightly as the ropes did.

Silence is critically important. Or, more precisely, *my* silence is critically important. I knew that from day one. Inordinate efforts, overt and covert, went into shutting me up. Teachers rewarded quiet children. My mother told me if I didn't have anything nice to say not to say anything at all, and she meant it. The priests who routinely ripped my body and mind apart held knives to my throat and told me they'd kill me if I ever said a word. My father tolerated me best when he had me muzzled.

All systems of oppression—from child abuse to racism to ableism—function most effectively when victims don't talk. Silence isolates, keeps us focussing inward rather than outward, makes perpetrators' work easier, confuses and overwhelms. I didn't know this as a child and teenager. I just knew I had to be quiet. The few times I managed to croak something truthful, I experienced repercussions, swift and brutal, that left no doubt about my oppressors' intentions.

I take speech seriously. This revolutionary action often comes with severe consequences. Speaking out carries danger, and not in abstract, theoretical ways. Telling the truth can't be taken lightly, or engaged in glibly.

At the same time that I understand this, I want to speak. Through those brutal decades, the part of me that wants to talk—and talk honestly—somehow survived, and now gains strength daily. That part of me propels me to the desk, picks up a pen, pushes me to write honestly, to write in spite of fear, because of fear. It refuses to let me live out my life bowing to the dictates of perpetrators and accomplices who tried to destroy me.

public persona and privilege

Audience members at the reading don't sense my terror, because I'm an expert at hiding feelings and functioning in the face of unmitigated disaster. If I wasn't so afraid, I'd be amused at the gap between their perceptions and my reality. Someone asks a question about my fiction. I say: "Characters show up in my head and start talking and I try to write it down. These characters are often gregarious and talk loudly. So far I like all the characters who have arrived on the scene, except for some minor ones."

The audience perceives some radical leap of creative artistic energy on my part and is impressed. I consider a street person approaching any of these people and daring to speak about people in her head. The audience member would walk away as quickly as possible, after labeling the street person crazy. No audience member knows I've been labeled crazy and locked up in a psych ward. Would it change their opinion of my creative artistic energy if they did? But I can't know the answer, because fear locks up my lips.

I don't want to minimize my terror, but neither do I want to dwell on that alone, ignoring my fulfillment and privilege. Writing excites me. Fiction comes from characters who appear out of nowhere and *talk* to me. I wake up with the first two lines of a poem on my lips. I can't get ideas down fast enough when writing analytical essays. My fingers itch, and I place them on the computer keyboard as often as I can. This cultural work satisfies me; no adult I knew as a child got this from daily work.

And I can't forget I have a kitchen with food in it, writing utensils, clothes. These are privileges. They should be rights for everyone on the planet, but right now they're privileges and I must think about how I use them. Another of my privileges—which should also be a right—is literacy, the ability to read and write and express myself. I grew up around people who could not do this, and I understand the internal frustration and social scorn illiteracy evokes. Sharing class location with an illiterate person doesn't mean our experiences mirror each other's. In this case, I experience a privilege she is denied.

So, how do I handle my privileges? Do I espouse the oppressive lie about "pulling myself up by my bootstraps," and insist that if I can get my words published, anyone can? Or do I understand my literacy and writing skill as one tool for resistance and liberation? Why do I write? For who, for what? Who benefits?

resistance and love

No one told me, as a child, that the first writing system and alphabet emerged from what is now the Arab world, about Arabs creating algebra, about the amazing Arabic traditions of literature, story-telling, poetry, and philosophy, about the working-class history of political action and critical thinking, about great working-class storytellers who blend humor and sadness. I know these things now; activist work (my own and others') opened up a world of historical and cultural information that changed my life. Slowly and painfully, I've come to believe working-class people of color, including myself, have important artistic/theoretical contributions to make. This simple truth proved powerful and liberating. It doesn't solve every problem or eradicate oppression, but it makes an enormous difference in my daily life. Without it, I couldn't write.

When I believe my life has meaning, believe it enough that I write down life experiences and my analyses of them, I resist oppression. Each piece of writing, whether analytical essay, poem, or fiction, contradicts lies about working-class people of color: we can't think critically, we're too enmeshed in life's dreary necessities to create art, our mundane lives can't possibly generate interesting material.

My writing results from this desire to resist; it stems from deep feelings of love and caring—for people in my communities, for dogged survivors who refuse to succumb to forces wearing them down day after day, for the ones who've generated beauty in spite of incredible hardship, for the wise, articulate, sweet people I grew up with who disappeared quietly into the night because they were too yellow and too poor.

final words

Writing this essay terrified me. At times fear prevented me from seeing the words on the page. *Who do you think you are? How dare you open your mouth? Have you forgotten what we can do to you?* Part of me still believes speaking the truth is dangerous, foolhardy, and a recipe for disaster, still believes I'm worthless and stupid. Oppressors burned these messages into my brain and beat them into my body, and it's hard to get rid of them. Only with a supportive community, a political analysis, and love am I coming to perceive myself as an artist and creator who can move through debilitating fear.

And so I say to other working-class writers of color: for ourselves and all those still terrified and terrorized, we must take ourselves and our work seriously. We must treat ourselves with respect and care, believe in each other, understand the forces aligned against us, hold out hope in a world that teaches us despair, refuse to live out our time on earth as passive victims, understand the power and magic of words and how they heal. The ancestors wait. My ancestors wait for me to claim my place as a working-class Arab halfbreed queer girl who loves to think and write and does it purposefully and creatively. Your ancestors wait for you to seize power. Let the waiting time be short.

notes

1. Thanks to Jan Binder and Juliana Pegues for their help with this essay.

Working-Class Culture

not an oxymoron

clicking on the keys

My Aunt Rose always had a whiskey within reach, smoked copiously, caked on the makeup, and wore so many bracelets she sounded like a rhythm section when she walked or, rather, teetered in her high heels. Her laugh could be heard three houses away. She refused to take off her sunglasses inside church, and fell asleep the moment the sermon began. Aunt Rose cooked and consumed huge amounts of Lebanese food, and loved to dance the debke.[1] A talented pianist, she taught neighborhood children, played the organ at church every Sunday, and led our extended-family sing-alongs. I can still hear and see her clearly—long, painted fingernails clicking on the piano keys, whiskey and water within reach, raspy voice singing whatever song we clamored to hear. "Secondhand Rose" was always a big hit:

> Secondhand Rose
> I'm wearing secondhand clothes
> on Second Avenue
> Even Jake the plumber
> he's the man I adore
> had the noive to tell me
> he'd been married before...

Back then I didn't connect these activities to art or culture because I'd been indoctrinated with classist beliefs. My working-class family had no culture, no artistic gifts. Our Arab-ness made us a tad more interesting than our white neighbors, but even this "exotic" element couldn't outweigh class limitations and constraints. Like every other kid on the block, I knew that the general motors executive, in suit and tie, escorting his wife to the concert hall for an evening of classical music was participating in a cultural event. The common-law heterosexual couple packing their kids, and the neighbors' kids, into a beat-up pick-up truck to attend a local square dance got sneers for being "such hillbillies,"[2] even if they didn't live anywhere near the hills.

What I learned simply mirrored dominant beliefs: Rich people have culture, poor people don't. This is expressed in various ways, sometimes by advancing the idea of a split between arts and crafts, between high art and low art. Functional and accessible "crafts," no matter how beautiful, just can't compare with the expensive stuff safely locked away in a museum with a $10 admission charge.

the working-class person as an artist

Social-change activists from the 1950s through the '80s affected what's seen in museums, what's played on airwaves, and who's on stage. Today we reap the benefits of incredibly hard work done by people of color and/or women and/or working-class/poor people and/or queers[3] who organized and fought to open up the narrow parameters of public cultural expression.

These activists/artists met with tremendous resistance. Cultural arbiters with institutional power had no interest in hanging Black women's quilts in museums or hearing Arab music in community orchestra halls. They dug in their heels, were polite and rude in turn, but kept saying no. Some activists continued to push on that front, while others opened galleries, held concerts, and planned exhibitions. As we established more community spaces, we also gained access to some museum walls and some prestigious stages.

Forced to include some of our art, curators and art "experts" had to figure out what to call it. They hadn't been faced with this before, since rich white men's art is just art. They came up with two categories—"traditional" and "ethnic." There are a couple of interesting points here. First, they held onto the power of classifying art/culture—they maintained hegemony over the power of naming. Second, their choice of "traditional" and "ethnic" merits examination.

These terms aren't total misrepresentations or totally inappropriate. "Traditional" captures the notion of an ongoing cultural activity that carries a long history. "Ethnic" clearly refers to artwork done by people of color, whether African, Native, Latino, or Asian (including Arab). In this race-conscious society, the term has the potential to interrupt the common and problematic practice of making people of color and our cultures invisible. But when used as *the* two definitive categories, "traditional" and "ethnic" skew reality. These categories appear to be mutually exclusive; they are not. Further, they position class outside the discussion's boundaries, keeping working-class and working-poor identities of particular artists hidden.

These categories allow the social silence around working-class/working-poor culture to continue. Art by poor white people is called traditional, a term often used to define quilts, carpentry, country-western music, and doll-making. Art by poor people of color (recent or long-term immigrants or Native Americans)[4] is described as ethnic art, whether located in fine-arts museums or natural-history museums. Everything from Hmong embroidery to Arab tile-making, from Yoruba music to Indonesian dance, falls into this category.

But the idea that valid, life-enhancing cultural expressions come from working-class people, whether "ethnic" or "American," still falls outside most people's conceptual framework. That idea can't fit into the narrow categories set up by self-appointed definers of culture, nor can it exist within elitist belief systems that insist poor people have no culture. Consequently, there's been little public interest to date in Joe Schmoe factory worker who has spent twenty years using watercolor paintings to document work on the line; he's not creating traditional art and can't be relegated to an ethnic group because he's white.

Cultural arbiters have decided they'll use our quilts, our music, and our embroidery only when defined and packaged according to their specifications. This leaves out huge numbers of artists like my Aunt Rose, whose cultural work couldn't be packaged or defined appropriately. Everything she did was too clearly and visibly working-class. Suppose someone showed interest in her ability to teach and lead the debke. They'd soon realize their mistake. Horrid presentation! Instead of a suitably modest, traditional Arab dress with intricate embroidery, or a suitably sexy belly-dancing outfit with cleavage showing, Aunt Rose wore lavish makeup, high heels, and short skirts, and backcombed her dyed, jet-black hair very high. Let's try something else. Hmm. Nix on the traditional category; she didn't embody the characteristics of the quiet, modest, working-class woman smiling sweetly while giving piano lessons to lovely little children. Instead, she dragged on cigarette after cigarette while she taught, and her incredibly long, brightly-painted fingernails tapped cheerily on the keys. (I didn't learn until later that "serious" piano players find this completely unacceptable.) Well, what about her ability to play from memory all the popular songs from the '40s and '50s, and to lead sing-alongs? Another no-go. According to restrictive definitions for ethnic art, a Lebanese woman singing "Secondhand Rose" with a full glass of whiskey and water beside her wasn't doing anything Arab. Especially with snow outside.

I believe present-day artists/activists must push past the static, false categories of traditional and ethnic, and broaden our definitions of art/culture. Class must inform our political work around culture; we need to become aware of how class integrates itself into cultural expression. Let's focus on artists' class identity and include art by working-class/working-poor people, of color and white. Shaping our work with this awareness will profoundly affect our political organizing, and allow us to create and follow guiding principles that more accurately reflect our identities and communities.

art that turns my stomach

Do I think all working-class art is great? No. A lot of it falls into the "awful" category, along with so much middle-/upper-class art. By awful, I don't mean "ugly" or "unattractive." Ugly art can be emotionally disturbing, carry strong meaning and speak clearly about particular people and issues. That's not a problem. For me, awful art exhibits a lack of personal connection to its creator or its creator's community, means nothing to the artist, and may have been thrown together solely for cash or prestige (and I'm not criticizing the few working-class people who manage to make a living producing something rich people want to buy).

Class membership doesn't ensure awful art or good art. Class membership does ensure whose art, whose cultural expression, is valued and appreciated. Any talk about class and art necessarily entails talk about critics and criticism. Not surprisingly, the white, upper-middle-class sensibilities that have traditionally dominated the critics' world are unimpressed by and even hostile to working-class art and artists. Thus, awful art by upper-middle-class artists receives praise and legitimacy, while impressive art clearly exhibiting working-class form and content is passed over without comment, or has its many "flaws" scrupulously documented.

This is one reason social-change activists must involve ourselves in criticism, must respond to cultural work from a place of understanding class. Because I know about working-class/working-poor beliefs, values, and sensibilities regarding art and culture, I perceive more in our art than an upper- or middle-class critic who has no interest in moving outside the boundaries set by her profession. For example, I understand the importance we place on accessible arts and culture. I also know this ethic is completely at odds with the standards evoked by western art critics, and that working-class/working-poor people don't have the social and political power to implement this ethic anywhere except our own communities.

Those in power in our society have always asserted that art available to everyone isn't much good. According to capitalist ideology, rare, hard-to-find art—which is in part rare and hard-to-find because of the art industry's organizing principles—is more valuable than common, easy-to-find art. Thus prices can be raised and profit margins pushed over the top. The making of rare, limited-edition prints (excuse me, but does anyone else find the term "limited edition" a bit pretentious for "not making any more copies"?) pays off again and again.

This makes sense within a capitalist framework, where profit is the key motivating factor. A whole set of meanings around particular items must be established and enacted. An industry of art dealers, art investors, and art "experts" backs up these ideas and puts them into practice.

The social construction of rarity[5] is one of the operating principles behind institutionalized art standards. While capitalism didn't invent the idea of coveting rare art, it has developed and strengthened the concept to the point where the scrawl of a well-known artist on a small scrap of paper can bring in hundreds of thousands of dollars. Industry support seems to be equally or more important than talent in determining price.

While one segment of the market focuses on rare editions, another runs rampant with mass productions. Limitless, as opposed to limited, editions of paintings of flowers and cute white children are churned out day after day. Ceramic objects, glitzy wall decorations, and colored photographs of mountains can be had cheaply; this art for the masses is as carefully marketed and just as removed from the creative impulse as "rare" editions.[6] While mass-produced items bring in less profits, the quantity sold helps even the scales. Both segments of the market focus on profit. Neither is interested in the liberatory potential of art created by the people for the people.

joining in even when you don't want to

As I was driving home late one night from the queer country-western bar my lover and I frequent, an image of a ballet dancer popped into my head and I started thinking about the differences between two-stepping and ballet. A partnered dance done to country-western music, two-stepping involves taking two slow steps in time to the beat, followed by two quick steps. It's easy to learn (if hard to do well), and most people grasp the basics in one night. A dancer of average talent can teach others. Lessons are usually free or inexpensive.

My mind jumped from here to one of the earliest dances I learned—the debke.[7] After getting lessons from Aunt Rose, I watched, over the years, as she taught debke steps to new people who joined our extended-family gatherings. She insisted everyone dance—young or old, on crutches, shaky limbs, or healthy legs, it didn't matter. Time and again, Aunt Rose simply ignored protests based on age, ill health, or two left feet, and pulled people into the circle. While it takes time, skill, and commitment to do the debke well, usually people only need one lesson to reach a generalized skill level. One lesson from Aunt Rose offered that.

My aunt wanted everyone to participate because the debke can't be done alone, the party goes better if everyone's having fun, and dancing's more enjoyable than sitting on the sidelines. No money or special equipment was required, nor extra space; a church hall, a living room, a backyard sufficed. Aunt Rose praised all dancers, advanced and beginning. Differing skill levels didn't cause problems, because the activity's parameters are wide enough to incorporate differences. The ratio of women to men didn't matter, since it's a group dance without sex/gender divisions or heterosexual coupling.

Contrast this dance form with ballet. Outrageous admission prices,[8] highly gendered movement sequences, and the average person's inability to participate mark ballet as a middle- and upper-class art form. I don't want to trash ballet dancers, most of whom work very hard for little money and are themselves commodified; I want to analyze dance forms from different classes. For ballet, lots of money is needed for shoes, rental space, teachers' fees, and outfits. Costs for lessons are prohibitive, in part because it takes so long to learn. Few potential ballet dancers have an Aunt Rose available to teach basic skills in the living room. Instead, a specialized teacher must be found, and the more advanced the student, the more difficult the search.

Most people don't continue with ballet lessons because of difficulty and expense. Only the most determined will press on and "make it" in the highly-competitive and stressful world of the middle- and upper-class art scene. Once lessons or expert-monitored rehearsals stop, ballet stops, since it's not a dance you can partake in sporadically.

In a sense, differences between debke and ballet generally capture differences between art/culture created and engaged in by rich people and poor people. Poor people are looking for group participation; rich people often chase performance and star status. Ballet dancers train for years in hopes of performing in high-priced venues; debke dancers and two-steppers are usually happy dancing once a week with friends.

the artist as a working-class person

Exciting cultural work is emerging from marginalized communities, as we identify ourselves and each other, celebrate our cultures, discover our histories, resist oppression, struggle for liberation. One important aspect of our work is encouraging artistic and cultural expressions among group members. But how do we talk about class? Class differences mark significant splits among, for example, racial/ethnic groups. In and of themselves, these differences don't need to weaken or divide us. Weakening and division come when differences aren't acknowledged and taken seriously, when our own thinking about art and culture doesn't consider class.

Activists/artists have worked for years to create openings for art from marginalized communities. I'm intent on continuing this work, adding class awareness to organizing efforts, and bringing artists like Aunt Rose into the foreground. It's up to us to ensure community members don't get left behind, scorned, and belittled. The task of asking critical questions about art and culture, and insisting the class location of the artist matters, remains with those of us who started these discussions—cultural workers marginalized on the basis of our race, gender, sexuality, immigrant status, class, language. To do this, we need a strong and critical understanding of all aspects of our identities.

For example, within Arab-American communities there are a variety of types of artistic expression. Some of us, usually recent immigrants, create art that strongly reflects the land we just left. Others, whose families immigrated several generations ago, usually create art that is some conglomeration of aesthetics from the country in which we live, our class location, and our family's country of origin. This doesn't mean the art of the second group is less Arab-American—unless we make the mistake of setting up rigid categories of what qualifies as Arab within our own communities. In that case, artists like my Aunt Rose, whose creative outlets wove together reflections of life in a new country, her class experiences, and Lebanon, would be left out.

giving Aunt Rose the last laugh

My Aunt Rose had a great sense of humor, a trait she shared with almost every working-class person I know. Humor holds an honored place as a long-lived form of working-class cultural expression that helps us survive and stay sane. It's a polished art form in our communities, and comes through not only in jokes but in music and storytelling. Both a critique of capitalism and a mild sense of self-deprecation run through our humor.

Aunt Rose told funny stories, about inept bosses complaining about her fingernails tapping on typewriter keys, about piano students who didn't know the difference between the treble clef and the bass clef, about messing up a batch of grapeleaves, about winning at poker and losing at bridge. After sharing these stories, she'd throw back her head and let loose with a raucous series of shrieks, slapping her thigh at the same time. Through all the crap she took as an Arab, a woman, a working-class person who labored as a secretary from the age of fifteen, she held that sense of humor close. In light of what I now know about class oppression, I connect her jokes to her art and perceive Aunt Rose as a working-class artist who let humor permeate her work, who never took herself too seriously, who added laughter to every sing-along and every debke lesson.

Aunt Rose died too young, reduced to skin and bones in a cold hospital room. Cancer, which continues to ravage working-class people of color, cut her down in her sixties. The disease attacked so quickly that I, living in another city, had no chance to say a real good-bye. When I reached her bedside, her mind was gone, and the stocky body that reflected our peasant roots in the same way mine does had wasted away to nothing.

We'd had our last real conversation several months earlier, after I'd been arrested for committing civil disobedience at a plant manufacturing parts for the cruise missile. Aunt Rose and I munched pretzels while curled up on her bright green and yellow couch, TV playing low in the background. I told her the whole story, hoping for an encouraging response; Aunt Rose didn't let me down.

"*They* arrested *you!*" she squawked. She threw back her head with the dyed black hair and let loose with those raucous shrieks. "They arrested you!" she repeated in the familiar tone that managed to mix disgust for them and approval for me. "Now that's a good one."

notes

1. Traditional Arab folk dance.
2. Hillbillies, a term simply referring to people living in a hilly or backwoods region, has taken on an excessively negative meaning because of anti-rural and anti-working-class oppression.
3. I use "and/or" to make it clear that people belong to one or more of these groups. Some people belong to all of these groups.
4. Non-Anglo "white" people, such as Sephardic Jews, also get put in this category.
5. Jan Binder coined the phrase and explained the idea of the social construction of rarity. She gave me a great deal of help in figuring out how to frame this essay, and this particular section. Jeff Nygaard provided further important ideas for this section. Thanks to him and Marjorie Huebner for their editing help.
6. I don't believe *all* high-priced paintings are uninspired but am trying to make sense of how they fit into the capitalist framework.
7. Interestingly, the debke and two-stepping have many things in common.
8. There is something hilarious about rich people paying upwards of $40 to watch from the sidelines while gay men throw too-skinny women in the air.

Looking Back

You drifted lazily from the sky,
touched down
in that loneliest of organs.
We probed through scarred hearts,
thickened from the war years.

For the first time,
I didn't finish my sentences.
You spoke my secret language
of east moved to west
stopped at factory door.

Only a week and you drifted again,
no piece of anchor handed over.

Later,
another scar formed
on my left ventricle
as your tongue
made a wide detour
around my name.
No surprises for me;
I've spent too many years
on the front line.

Look all ways,
dart into that
one patch of open space,
grab these five long minutes
before the bombs plummet again.

Make the connection. Run.
Leave no trace
of this furtive meeting
under the night sky.

Parents wanted faces kept forward.
They leapt from the east
landed clumsily in the west
your mama sprawling face down
my father on his back.

They warned us:
Looking back means remembering.
Remembering guarantees
finding stories.
Finding stories translates
into feeling a broken tongue.
Feeling a broken tongue
equals residing with bodily harm.
Residing with bodily harm
is the life of an Arab transplant.

Who can bear it?
Who can live
with a heart wide open?
Surely not us,
our marked hunks
of gnarled muscle
beating slowly.

When the shelling ceased
you opened for one brief moment,
let the sun from my stilted words
warm you,
then you vanished
into the future
without a backward glance.

Not me.
I peer over my shoulder.
Your shadow glides into my foreground.
Memories return.
Your face in my dream.
I retrieve scraps of paper.
Buried deep in desert sand.
I feel your broken tongue.
Kiss my purple lips.
I live with bodily harm.
You'll never look back.

I've always known the life
of an Arab transplant.
The heart is a lonely organ.

Catholic School Days

sketch number one

*I*n grade school I learned that Christopher Columbus discovered North America and that Anthony Dell is going to jail. Later I learned only one of these statements was true.

Deep divisions cut through that catholic schoolyard, and it still hurts to remember the lessons we learned so young. We skipped rope and smoked cigarettes and played spin-the-bottle together. But even through our no-tongue kisses, divisions remained. We knew where each of us was headed. If class possibilities aren't up front from day one, some of us might get the wrong idea. Close my eyes, recite the litany:

The Dell boys are headed for jail. Wendy Reilly will get pregnant and drop out of school, soon. So will Suzanne Beaulieu. So will a whole host of girls; their names alone would fill page after page. The Newton kids are borderline; Martin doesn't have a chance but the girls' looks might get them through high school. Then again, those looks might ensure pregnancy. Donny, jail, no question. Me and my friend Carla Beneditto, we'll make it through high school without getting pregnant (not true), then get jobs, secretaries if lucky. Inez Fournier will never graduate from high school, and never have a boyfriend. Margy Mitchell will teach, she might even leave town. David Custer and Liz Allen are set for university. A desk at the city's reform school has Maria Kane's name on it; she'll arrive there after she's forced to give her baby up for adoption. Russell Leblanc and Joey Rutger are going to get hooked on drugs, Kathy Connelly will end up poorer and skinnier than she already is. If that's possible.

A general motors city. Population 35,000. At first glance, class divisions seem obvious. Dad works on the line, or Dad works in the office. The divisions are that simple, and they are not. Imagine the boulders lining Somerset Creek; one shade moves into another, deep brown fades into brown slips into light gold echoes to yellow. Imagine class divisions so intricate, so delicate, so real, so jagged.

Imagine Anthony and me, both tough as nails hard as rocks with soft flannel and cinnamon sugar underneath. Imagine Anthony and me connecting across and through our hardness and softness, recognizing each other through rocks and nails, talking to each other but never with words. Imagine Anthony and me with a world plunked down between us. Not because of his white skin and my yellow skin, but because of the union. My father happened to be in the right place at the right time.

My father grew up poor, never finished high school, had a succession of lousy, dangerous jobs that ended suddenly because of a boss's whim. Then he got taken on at the motors. He held the job until the birth of the UAW.

I liked the union. It meant my dad couldn't be fired because the boss had a bad day. He probably wouldn't get killed in a factory accident. He got paid every Friday. When the bosses laid off the workers, which they did a lot, the union paid them from a common fund. The factory was relatively clean. My dad got regular breaks and could go to the bathroom when he needed. He got paid for overtime.

Anthony Dell's father grew up poor, never finished high school, had a succession of lousy, dangerous jobs that ended suddenly because of a boss's whim. He didn't get taken on at the motors. He just ended up at more lousy, dangerous jobs. Then he left his wife and their four boys, each spaced a year apart. They never saw him again.

Two years older than me, Anthony ended up in my Grade 7 class because he had failed twice. We didn't enter Grade 8 together because he flunked Grade 7. After that, he rarely showed up.

This is what Anthony Dell looked like: short and stocky. Hands as wide as they were long. I held hands with him during games, and his hands felt dry and chapped, like they needed lotion but his mom couldn't afford it. He had brown eyes, freckles, and tousled light-brown hair that he never combed. Tough as nails hard as rocks. Wearing large, faded flannel shirts and patched work pants and workboots, all worn by his three older brothers.

Me: short and stocky. Hands as wide as they were long. Brown eyes, yellow skin, long braids. Tough as nails hard as rocks. Wearing handmade navy skirts and white blouses and too-large coats, all worn by my older sister and cousins.

I was on a serious search and so was Anthony—an ever unsuccessful search for softness. We couldn't even imagine it but kept looking anyway. A hole in the ground would do, as long as it offered momentary rest from the daily fight for breath. Softness must live somewhere, could we survive without it, would we ever stumble across it?

The Dell boys were headed for jail. Even though they did nothing the rest of us didn't. They skipped school, they swore, they smoked, they shoplifted. I didn't skip school, because I liked school better than home, but I swore, I smoked, I shoplifted. Wendy Reilly smoked, didn't shoplift, her stomach got big in Grade 8, and she disappeared. Suzanne Beaulieu shoplifted, smoked, and laughed a lot before she got pregnant and dropped off the face of the earth. Inez Fournier's sister died an unnecessary death but Inez did not look surprised. Martin Newton faded out of sight, two of his sisters got pregnant within months of each other, two graduated from high school and worked as secretaries. David Custer shoplifted, smoked, swore, skipped school but knew enough to bring forged notes, and we knew his destination. Liz Allen, also on her way to higher education, initiated every game of spin-the-bottle we ever played, smoked like a trooper, had the stickiest fingers of all. Except, of course, Josie Hughes, who never left a store without $100 worth of goods in her pockets and up her skirt, who talked very fast and very much, smoked cigars, and had the same kind of home life I did. I can't say for sure about her.

Probably a cruddy apartment, on welfare, with kids. With a man who does the same things her father did.

Our Grade 7 teacher, Sister Ann Richard, gave us a homework assignment. Pick a topic, read, research, write a five-minute speech, practice, memorize, present it to the class. Everyone groaned. I looked at Anthony. He was failing, partly because he never did his homework. I couldn't imagine him writing a speech.

Sister Ann called on Anthony Dell sixth, after Liz Allen, Suzanne Beaulieu, Carla Beneditto, Kathy Connelly, and David Custer. Anthony shuffled to the front of the class, uncombed hair, chapped hands, workboots, red and black flannel shirt. He held no paper in his hand and my stomach sank. But I needn't have worried. Anthony proceeded to deliver the best speech we heard. Everyone's eyes were riveted on him. We remembered that speech for years, because Anthony Dell, tough as nails hard as rocks, sweet as cinnamon sugar, soft as worn flannel, unbolted the padlock across his heart and offered two minutes of access. None of us had ever loosened that bolt, none of us except Anthony Dell, one of the Dell boys, headed for jail.

"The best thing to do if you wanna know about the animals is to go and sit in the woods and just wait. Just wait. You gotta wait a long time and not be in a hurry. You can't smoke or nothin, can't talk, just gotta sit on an old tree stump and wait for them. It's their home, you're just visitin and so you gotta wait.

"I like to go back behind Somerset crick, in them woods by a little stream that cuts off from the crick. I sit and sit, just waitin. Then I'll see a groundhog, a big ol groundhog, scurryin around, lookin for food. They're really big."

Anthony held his chapped hands a foot apart. We all stared, wide-eyed.

"Then I hear a noise. I look behind me. Quick as you can, this little brown bunny scoots across the path. Two jumps and it's down into a hole. Can't even see that hole, the rabbit hid it so good. Poof! It's gone.

"I sit and sit, and you gotta be okay about just sittin, no noise no nothin, just waitin and waitin. You hear birds twitter

in the trees, you see a bunch of leaves fall off the branches and you think, if I was an animal, I'd just live out here right under this tree. I'd dig me a little hole where it'd be nice and dark and warm and I'd just pop in there, poof, like the rabbit.

"I like animals. I think them's real nice. Nicer than people, a lotta them. I don't wanna hunt. I just wanna watch them and maybe pet 'em if they let me. Once I sat a real long time and this rabbit, it just looked at me and sat beside me for a while, like we was friends. I watched it and I couldn't even see its eyes blink, it just stared with big brown eyes. It looked at me, like it was okay for me to be sittin there, it liked me. I looked at the rabbit. We just sat for a real long time."

Dead silence. Then loud applause and a few whistles. Anthony turned beet red, tilted his head sideways and scuttled back to his chair. Sister Ann gave him a C because he talked for two minutes instead of five, but all of us knew who had given the best speech. I looked at my friend. How do padlocks across hearts come unbolted? Would mine ever be? What about Suzanne's, or Martin's? I wondered all of these things and I saw Anthony back at his desk, tousled hair dropping over red face, and I thought: this boy does not have a chance.

And I cry now, because I can, because I don't have to be tough as nails hard as rocks, I cry for these truths we learned in catholic grade school. I can see Anthony Dell in jail, chapped hands, uncombed hair, faded prison garb—not quite fitting, worn by three older brothers—surrounded by other soft sweet boys whose softness and sweetness got buried and no one's trying to dig it up. I think about our friendship, about softness and sweetness underneath rocks and nails, and I think about the world plunked between us because my father had been in the right factory at the right time and his had not. And I weep for a world whose divisions are clearly understood by children and whose chasms only get wider and no one seems to care.

This is what I learned in grade school: Anthony Dell is going to jail.

Stupidity
"Deconstructed"[1]

ozens of workers move deliberately around the building site at the University of Minnesota, driving huge machines, handling dangerous equipment, carrying heavy loads. They can barely talk over the noise, but they are communicating and working together well. A wrongly-interpreted nod, a misunderstood word, a petty quarrel could mean the loss of a hand or a life. Although that's not the only reason for cooperative efforts; they're a common working-class practice.

I connect with these workers. I've lived with people like them, worked with people like them—I'm one of them. The worst jobs I've had were made bearable thanks to our jokes, camaraderie, easy flow of conversation. The familiar sweat, dirty hands, missing teeth, and lined faces reassure me. Workers.

Workers at the university. We've built every university that has ever existed, yet we're shunned and despised within academia's hallowed halls. Explicitly and implicitly, we've been taught our place—and it's not in a student's desk or the professors' lounge. We're needed to construct the university, maintain, clean, and repair it.

Oh, we're welcome here, as long as we stay where we're supposed to. We know the monster that presents itself if we dare step out of place. *Stupid. We are too stupid to study, learn, think, analyze, critique. Because working-class people are stupid.* So much energy goes into the social lie that poor people are stupid; capitalism needs a basic rationalization to explain why things happen the way they do. So we hear, over and over, that our lousy jobs and living situations result from our lack of smarts. I internalized this lie. Rationally, I knew money and brains didn't go hand in hand. But on deep unconscious levels, I believed in my own stupidity and in the stupidity of working-class people.

I want to examine these dynamics in this essay which I titled "Stupidity 'Deconstructed'" in order to connect with construction workers *and* to express my irritation toward postmodernists who consistently use the term. This piece goes hand in hand with the writing of working-class people committed to theorizing about our experiences in universities and factories. It's past time for such a movement; *we* must create theory about our lives. No one else. If middle- and upper-middle-class people want to write about indoctrination into class privilege and unlearning it, great. But leave the rest to us.

A sordid history lurks here. Middle- and upper-middle class academics have traditionally sought out the experiences and stories of working-class/working-poor people for use in shaping theory. That is, we provide the raw material of bare facts and touching stories; they transform these rough elements into theory. Sound familiar? Gosh, it sounds like an exact replication of factory activity. Academics have approached me after I've given presentations on class, and said, "The stories about your family are so *interesting.*" *(Oh, thank you so much.)* "Don't you think they'd be stronger if you let them stand on their own?" Unedited translation: give me your stories, I'll write the theory. Leave it to the experts. *It's time to forget that shit.*

yes, i'm a worthy person, i have two university degrees.

I understand the workings of universities. I paid attention when I studied at the University of Toronto and the Episcopal Divinity School in Massachusetts. I've hung out on other campuses, and heard more than enough university stories. Levels of elitism and arrogance vary with regional difference, size, prestige, and how many misfits end up on the campus, but the core system remains: privileged people belong here.

If only I'd known this years ago! Then anger, instead of feeling crazy, alienated, and stupid, would have been uppermost. *Don't get me started. Even hearing that word makes my blood boil. Even hearing the word "smart" makes my blood boil. I want to wring your neck.*

From a young age, I loved to read and write and learn. But my future in that general motors city had been mapped out, and books didn't appear anywhere. I didn't like the map; nor did I like being surrounded by people who treated me like a handy repository for muddy boots and unmitigated rage. University offered a good solution (or so I thought). I started working paid jobs at age ten and saved every penny for the endeavor.

In Mr. Smythe's math class, the third floor of that ancient high school, sun streams through windows onto old wooden desks. Test results are read out loud—no surprises. Top marks for me, the Johnson twins, Brian Kingsley, Jonathon Woodley, Amanda Britian. Their label: brain. Mine: jock and party-er. Their parents: doctor, lawyer, psychiatrist, executive. Mine: line worker. Mr. Smythe advised the Johnson twins to apply to Waterloo or Toronto but not McMaster, and the intricacies of differences between these universities went way over my head; our guidance counselor poured over pamphlets and reference books with Brian once a week; Mr. and Mrs. Woodley and Jonathon drove to a different campus each weekend. I got wrecked every Friday and Saturday night and cruised around in cars driven by boys as stoned and drunk as me.

Despite my party-er status, despite the lack of help in selecting the "right" school, despite my total cluelessness, I applied to three universities. Only my grades appeared on transcripts; no entries for parents' work history or weekend activities. Fresh out of high school, naive but steadfast, I carried my cheap vinyl suitcase up those marble steps of Queen's University. Four months. I had cash for two years, but not enough class privilege. My throat locked, my tongue twisted, I sat in back rows with arms wrapped around chest and stomach. To say I felt like a fish out of water hardly describes my overwhelming feelings of confusion, depression, inadequacy, and shame. People actually asked me the year my grandparents graduated! Not just my parents, my *grandparents*. I thought everyone's grandparents were poor. I knew everyone's parents weren't poor, but I assumed everyone in the previous generation experienced poverty. Now rich white girls with straight teeth asked, "When did your grandparents graduate?" Four months. I'm surprised I lasted that long.

Years later I returned to those hallowed halls. Not through any formal, reasonable plan—more because I was pissed off. Today the whole thing strikes me as a big joke. During a bitter separation, a lawyer told me I could get more money from my ex-husband if I enrolled in university. During our marriage, I worked and supported him while he earned a degree, and I deserved an equivalent education. "Sounds good," I told her. We got the money and I went back to school.

Women's studies, University of Toronto. Middle-class and upper-middle-class women. *I'm so stupid.* I sat surrounded by women years younger than me, women exuding poise and confidence as they discussed graduate school options and Karl Marx. (Marx. Oh, yeah, that guy those other rich[2] people I worked with at CBC Radio used to spout off about.) *What am I doing here?* I talked to janitors and I talked to Kim, the last hold-out for cigarettes in the whole department. We scrunched in corners of the smoking lounge so she could indulge and the smoke gave me a headache, but I didn't care. Better a headache than crazy. Kim anchored me. A white girl, working-class, smart as a whip, skinny and tough. We sat close together in back rows and whispered comments to each other because we couldn't say them out loud. I couldn't have made it without her.

Another bizarre turn of events dropped me in graduate school. A professor at U of T actually took an interest in me. My brain flip-flopped. "You should go on to graduate school," she told me earnestly. "You're very smart. And you have such good study habits. You would do so well." Smart? No, stupid. Graduate school? No, janitor. What *is* graduate school? What happens there? What's an M.A.? A Ph.D.? They must be the same things with different names. I said nothing out loud; that would reveal my stupidity. A friend told me about a university with a master's program in feminist ethics. I didn't know any other graduate programs. I didn't know how to find them. *I can't believe I'm writing this down. Now people will know just how stupid I really am.* I didn't know jackshit.

I applied for the feminist ethics program and laid out stringent conditions to make it as unlikely as possible I would ever get there. *If* the school offered me acceptance, a scholarship covering tuition, a job on campus, housing for my lover and me. Then, and only then, would I take the leap. My divorce money had dried up, and I would never, never in a million years, take out a loan. I knew all about loans and debts. Every working-class person I grew up with laid down the law: never take out a loan for anything except a mortgage on a house. Loans are bad. Debts are bad. You'll never get rid of these horrible burdens. I'd fly to the moon before borrowing money for graduate school. *Graduate school. What is it?*

The school met my stringent conditions. Uh-oh. But once there, I found Joann and Sheri and Meck, and we laughed until we cried and cried until we laughed about academia and how stupid we felt. We didn't have Aristotle and Socrates as reference points, couldn't even spell the names. We didn't know how to use the library system. We hadn't grown up with parents and family friends waxing nostalgic about university days and cutesy pranks, thus easing our entry into this strange world.

Then, something truly amazing. A working-class professor. I studied with one of the most brilliant minds in this country, Dr. Katie Geneva Cannon, a working-class, African-American woman from the South, who pushed me and pushed me and pushed me to think critically about class. Take it apart, figure it out, analyze it, *it's just like my brother used to do when he started building stereo equipment at age ten*, pull and pull and pull, you are smart, she said, you need to write. I sat in class, sweating, tongue-tied, scared shitless, and looked at her, teaching, questioning, inspiring, her brilliance shining like a star. *She was destined to cook and clean for white people, that is, if she didn't get something worse—if she can do it, maybe I can too.*

Buildings cut from fine stone and beautiful wood. My hands ache with the remembering. The maintenance men I worked with: Tony, shy and sweet with a faint Portuguese accent; Al, tough hide covering a heart like worn flannel; Eddy, drifting from job to job, booze on his breath, twisted grin, broken front tooth. I worked with them through the summer and felt so comfortable in our little lounge, drinking coffee and smoking, smoking, always smoking—rich people have given it up but we're still puffing away.

I spent hours wrestling with voices in my head telling me "You're stupid," and listening to trusted friends telling me "You're not stupid. This system makes you feel stupid." We figured out our own analysis: the university system is intricately linked with the capitalist system. People with power at the university will do their part to reinforce and promote the capitalist explanation for class difference—smart rich people, stupid poor people—in return for continued benefits and privileges from the current structure. They don't want a motley bunch of upstart working-class urchins figuring any of this out and refusing to sit in quiet shame.

They don't want graduates of their system to end up like me: class identity and loyalties stronger than ever, angry about the others who never had a chance, who still believe they're stupid, who always will, some already in their graves. Yes, I'm angry.

constructing / deconstructing: building / hiring

For the capitalist system to continue ruthlessly grinding on (or for the capitalist system to "succeed," as you would say) those of us bred for stupid and/or dangerous work must believe we're not as smart as the people who boss us around. It's critical. Capitalism needs simple explanations about why poor people with lousy jobs take orders from men in suits. Lack of brains fits the bill. (So does the lie that rich people work harder. I'll tackle that in another essay.) Any noticeable class divisions stem from difference in intellectual capacity. Connected to this is the touting of "American ingenuity" as the doorway to upward mobility. It's as untrue as the existence of a whole class of stupid people, but if enough people believe it—even partially believe it—this idea will reinforce and strengthen capitalism. After all, if we believe brains lead to success, we'll blame ourselves for not getting ahead. Personal failure, not systemic oppression, explains why we're going nowhere so very fast.

I grew up learning the bulk of the population in our small general motors city—that is, workers—was stupid. Dumb, brutish, boring, close to animals. Did I believe it? In some ways, I knew people in my family had brains and the bosses didn't. My extended family joked about it frequently. But just as frequently, they indicated they believed it. And at deep levels, I internalized the lie and lived with it for years. It impacted my thoughts, decisions, and actions, and surfaced resoundingly when I entered university. The smugness and certainty with which upper-middle-class people paraded their brain cells jarred me; for a time I was taken in by this, and it contrasted so sharply with my inability to speak, let alone parade, that I felt I really must be stupid. Thankfully, that didn't last long. *Who knows what will happen if we realize that we're not so stupid and you're not so smart? Maybe you'll lose privileges and status. Maybe you'll have to clean up your own messes. Maybe we'll find fulfilling work and the drudge work will be shared equally. Maybe we'll remove your feet from our necks.*

Of course, I didn't feel stupid at university only because of constructions concerning stupid workers. That coupled with an unfamiliar upper-middle-class world made me feel stupid. I didn't know any of the middle-class/upper-middle-class reference points and contexts, ranging from GRE's and LSAT's to Ph.D.'s and post-doc fellowships. I couldn't swish around with the entitlement of privileged students; I crept. I liked janitors more than professors; more to the point, I identified with janitors, not professors.

Language proved crucially important in opening a door into clarity, awareness, and class pride. It happened this way: I grew up around people who built things—houses, additions on houses, large buildings. They talked about it by saying, "I built that." This meant they planned and designed something, then picked up a hammer, nails, and saw, and began constructing.

University professors used this same phrase, often when discussing summer homes. They said authoritatively, "I built that." I knew what it meant to build something and I thought they meant they must have built their summer home. But they didn't look like they knew anything about construction work. I felt confused. I was astounded when I stumbled across the translation. "I built this" really meant "I hired some of you to build this for me."

So. Privileged people misuse language in ways that distort meanings of commonplace, easy-to-understand words like "build." This told me something. Then I read articles focusing on class, usually written by university professors. I looked forward to these, because I needed to develop my class analysis and thought these articles would help. But again disappointment and shame resulted. I didn't understand most of what I read. Abstract and impersonal, these essays stood three times removed from concrete reality of working-class life.

After confusion and shame, another door opened. If they misused a simple word like build, how could I trust them? If their articles used weird words like "proletariat" and showed they didn't know the first thing about us, maybe they weren't quite so smart. *Maybe we weren't quite so stupid.*

My hunch solidified after examining academic attraction to and use of postmodern theory and language. This horrible mix of distorted language and casual appropriation of our ideas allowed me once and for all to dismiss the ideology about stupid workers. As far as I can tell, postmodern theoreticians say nothing new, but their inaccessible language makes it appear as though they do. For example, they're fascinated with the notion that multiple realities exist in society, and they've written and theorized extensively about this.

Puh-lease. Everybody in my neighborhood, including the mechanics who had to sniff carbon monoxide in tiny, enclosed garages all day long, grasped that idea with no problem. We lived it. We had our reality, the bosses had theirs, and we understood them both. Theorists like W. E. B. Du Bois wrote about double consciousness—whereby African Americans understand their reality and white people's—at the turn of this century. But I've never seen postmodernists attribute these ideas to the people of color and/or working-class people who've lived and understood them for centuries. Instead, postmodernists steal these ideas and dress them up in language so inaccessible only a tiny, elite group can discuss them.

We need to ask, and begin answering, hard, practical questions. Who defines smart and stupid, and why? Who misuses language, and for whose benefit? Who writes theory, and why? Who goes to university, and why? Who does the academy serve? Can universities be transformed into places where everyone is welcomed and respected?

In this country, the first institutions of higher learning were trade or agricultural schools and theological centers, with liberal arts colleges and medical schools following. Around the turn of this century, with the establishment of standardization and class-biased guidelines, universities took on the task of serving middle- and upper-class white men. That group enjoyed peace and quiet for several decades, until the rest of us began banging on the door. Grudgingly, after years and years of hard work, little chinks appeared in those thick, stone doors. *The doors we built, with our hands. The doors we couldn't walk through.* The misfits demanded entrance: Africans, Asians, Natives, Arabs, Latinos, women, queers, even welfare mothers. Even the sons and daughters of factory workers and miners and janitors. What's a rich white man to do? The stress must be unbelievable. Poor guys.

Capitalism exists as a human construct, not a natural or innate system. We've been steeped in lies about its inevitability, and it seems to take on its own life as its institutions reinforce each other and the system. But it *is* a human construct, carefully set up to keep a small number of people stretched out comfortably along the backs of the rest of us. Remember: human constructs can be destroyed.

rich equals smart, poor equals stupid

I think of the university and a swift hot anger rushes from the pit of my stomach, sweeps through my throat, bursts out of my mouth. Stone buildings beautifully carved, wooden rooms beautifully balanced. Underpaid exploited workers. Our hands next to the hands of a professor "deconstructing" ideas with strings of six-syllable words. *Stupid.* Underpaid exploited workers keeping these buildings clean. *Stupid.* I think of myself and working-class friends sitting in back rows, saying nothing, sweating, fearful that one word from these stubborn, hurt mouths will betray us, will expose our selves/our class.

Many mechanisms have been created in this rigidly defined, class-structured society to keep poor people in our place. Our place. We crouch over and the rest of you keep your feet on our necks. You sit complacently, feet resting comfortably—"Could you move just a little bit to the left?"—crossing ankles, smiling in our direction—"Very nice." One such mechanism is the constant, cross-racial image of the worker as stupid. Growing up, I attached "stupid" to workers and "smart" to executives. This didn't happen because of a weird personal quirk. It resulted from force-fed images and words of TV shows, newspapers, magazines, and movies. Any TV show with working-class characters, first "The Honeymooners" and "I Love Lucy," then "All In the Family," covertly and overtly highlighted the stupidity of bus drivers, factory workers, and plumbers. Movies, books, and comics followed suit. At school, middle-class kids called us stupid; we hurled back "stuck up," but never "stupid." Working-class/working-poor kids failed and dropped out, but not middle-class kids. Our town newspaper consistently portrayed general motors executives as calm, rational types, while union members appeared unthinking, wild, and chaotic.

Oh, you're exaggerating. You've gone too far. Stupid merely refers to someone not terribly intelligent. You've attached all these cultural, class-based meanings. You're way out on a limb. Chill out. People are gonna think you're nuts.

I look up "stupid" in the dictionary and find: 1. slow of mind, obtuse, brutish; 2. dulled in feeling or sensation, torpid; 3. marked by or resulting from dullness, senseless; 4. lacking interest or point, vexatious, exasperating.[3] I look up stupid in the dictionary and feel: 1. recognition; 2. affirmation of what I have felt my whole life and what I am saying in this essay; 3. fury; 4. disgust.

This dictionary definition fits precisely with what I learned in my bones before I could talk. A very particular set of cultural baggage goes along with stupid. Not a mere description of how well someone thinks, stupid has become a cultural concept with a particular code and set of signifiers that describe working-class people as the middle and upper classes perceive and construct us. It doesn't truthfully describe working-class people; rather, it speaks clearly to the particular understanding rich people created and maintain with a vengeance.

Brutish, dull, senseless. *I grew up believing we're thick-skinned, slow-witted, impervious to pain, boring.* The dominant culture drove this point home relentlessly. Someone called me sensitive and I couldn't grasp her meaning. *Working-class people can't be sensitive.* Rich people construct us as stupid and brainwash us Day One to make us believe it. We read their newspapers, watch their TV shows, take in their movies, and work jobs that reinforce what we see and hear. A vicious cycle.

What's the reality? I do know working-class people who fit the stereotype. Of course, their brains have been fried from decades of drudge work. Like Howie, my partner on the assembly line. Slow, barely able to get a complete sentence out of his mouth, unable to believe I learned his job in two hours. Vacant look, hollow eyes. Couldn't read. *You try working on an assembly line, at the same station, for thirty-eight years. How interesting will you be? How much will you know about world affairs? How creative will you feel?*

It's painful to acknowledge the fact that some of our brains have been fried. Not stupid from birth, as rich people insist, but fried from decades of the most boring, idiotic, repetitive work imaginable. I've done it. I fought every minute to keep my mind away from the hovering void. The boredom, lethargy, apathy, and meaninglessness surrounding that factory, surrounding every factory, constitutes a horrible and violating reality of daily life.

Stupid. They marked my family as stupid, and this confused me. I didn't think we were, but had no tools for arguing against such an intense social construct. I grew more confused and internalized the belief in my own stupidity, as all around me, my family proceeded with their lives and used their brains. My aunt went from grade school education to neighborhood CPA; she knew all the deductions, could add numbers ridiculously quickly, and did everyone's taxes for free. My grandfather, literate in three languages, poor, steered new Lebanese immigrants through the morass of landlords, bosses, lawyers. My father and uncles, with their tenth-grade educations, filled out daily crossword puzzles with pens and painstakingly planned, calculated, measured, added rooms on small houses, with wiring, plumbing, support beams, ceilings, floor tiles, never a sixteenth of an inch out. I once helped a friend build a porch, holding boards in place as she hammered, blinking in disbelief because half-inch gaps appeared. My mother and aunts balanced budgets, paying bills with nonexistent funds, borrowing some from here, begging some from there, adding and subtracting large numbers in their heads.

Class socialization begins early. Material possessions, home environment, and neighborhood provide information about our present situation and our future. Family members' sense of/lack of entitlement and expectation provides more. Social constructions of class, put out by institutions such as media and school, are a third factor. Whether family members resist or unquestioningly take in these social constructions impacts class socialization.

For a continuous supply of expendable workers, capitalism must offer ideas and experiences that reinforce each other. If people who look, act, talk, and live like you are constantly portrayed as working particular jobs because they're too stupid to get anything better, chances are you'll believe the lie when you end up in the same factory.

Ideas help reinforce and explain different class locations. Capitalism relies on various institutions, such as the university, to pass on relevant knowledge about the system. Universities need to replicate and reinforce central ideologies. Such as poor people stupid, rich people smart—a perfect example of the kind of polarized thinking that has hindered and weakened Western thought for centuries. These categorizations feed into an either/or mentality and ignore complications and complexities. They also shore up oppressive systems of racism, sexism, and classism because of the positive meaning attached to one half of the equation and the negative meaning attached to the other—male/female, white/black, heterosexual/homosexual, virgin/whore, thinking/feeling. I always include rich/poor and smart/stupid in this list of important categories; lately I've begun to perceive the ways they map on to each other to become rich smart/poor stupid.

In the years I spent in Women's Studies, we spent hours and hours analyzing the superficial nature of dualistic thinking around men/women, white/black, and thinking/feeling, and reflected on more complicated and realistic understandings. But we never touched on the smart/stupid, rich/poor breakdown. (Of course, we were in a university classroom.) This particular ideological split goes a long way to support the dangerous, classist myth I've discussed in this essay. It's time to pay attention.

In thinking about rich smart/poor stupid, we need to analyze stupidity and intelligence. Writing this essay might play into the belief that only one kind of intelligence exists, the kind defined and revered by the ruling class in conjunction with academics, because I focus on the university, the stupid/smart dichotomy, and class oppression. That's not my intention. In the same ways I understand the category of "race" as a myth while acknowledging the reality of racism and different physical/cultural traits, I want to put "intelligence" as defined in a limited and narrow way by the ruling class into the myth category, while acknowledging a variety of mental capacities and different types of intelligence.[4]

Many different kinds of intelligence exist, and these cross class lines. Universities revere the type of intelligence that can synthesize information rapidly and understand abstract concepts. Equally valid types of intelligence enable a child to design and build a bird house, a mother to balance a budget with no money, an "uneducated" man to enthrall listeners with stories, a young woman who hasn't had music lessons to compose a piano tune, a girl to write a poem, a homeless person to comprehend the poem, a neighborhood to devise a plan to stop a company from dumping toxic waste, three young women to invent scathing responses to catcalls and whistles. These types of intelligence require creativity, humor, ability to ask questions, care, a good memory, compassion, belief in solidarity, ability to project an image of something that doesn't physically exist.

Some manual-labor jobs require intelligent, creative thinking, such as carpentry, video technology, and grounds keeping/designing. Most manual-labor jobs require little thinking of any sort, and are marked by monotony and danger. Some executive jobs require intelligence and creative thinking, and most don't. (None, however, are likely to be dangerous.) On the whole, capitalism has offered little in the way of stimulating, educational, growth-enhancing work experiences.

can i really be working-class and smart?

The sarcasm in this heading is an attempt to get at underlying and often unconscious beliefs about stupidity which popped up constantly after I got my master's degree. People freaked out. Working-class people with university degrees freak out ourselves and our middle-class "brothers and sisters" (more sarcasm). We ask: "Am I still working-class?" Middle-class people inform us, delicately and sensitively: "You're not working-class anymore."

Where do these reactions come from? Let me first examine what working-class people mean when we say: *am I working-class now?* I have a university degree. A secret subtext, a critical message lurks here.

One day I figured out my translation. When I asked: "Am I working-class now that I have a university degree," I meant: "Am I working-class now that I'm smart?" Back to my theory about dualistic thinking. If the stupid/smart dichotomy is a cornerstone of the academy, and if this division rests clearly along class lines (rich people smart/poor people stupid) then conferring university degrees onto middle- and upper-class people isn't only about knowledge, courses passed, GPAs, degrees, and job security. University degrees constitute a symbol, a marker, so the world understands the bearer comes from the middle/upper-class. Degrees separate this group from lowly, unprivileged, stupid workers.

Then working-class people traverse the minefield of academia and end up with initials after our names. We get confused. Very confused, because those initials symbolize the separation between rich and poor. Rich people need these degrees to feel smart, to remind themselves they are not a lowly janitor sweeping halls, a lowly cook slopping out lousy cafeteria food. They need them, but somehow we end up with them. We get confused. Are we announcing we're smart? But working-class people can't be smart. *If we are working-class, we can't be smart. Therefore, since we've earned a university degree, we are no longer working-class.*

Now, that's not true, for at least three reasons. First, whatever is going on subconsciously, consciously I know rich people aren't necessarily smart. Having cleaned their houses, read their garbled manuscripts, and "typed" (code word for "re-wrote") their incoherent essays, I'm well aware of this.

Second, whatever silly initials my friends and I carry after our names, we're still working-class.[5] We still talk the same and feel the same and work shit jobs. We don't float around thinking we're entitled to everything; we don't grab whatever we want. We don't acquire privilege, entitlement, and arrogance after slogging it out in the academy.

Third, all of this begs the question: does class location change if one factor governing class location alters? Some people say yes. For them, once working-class people make a good salary they cease being working-class. By the same standard, if working-class people earn university degrees, they leave their class of origin.

I disagree with this, since I believe class identity comes from many places: education, values, culture, income, dwelling, lifestyle, manners, friends, ancestry, language, expectations, desires, sense of entitlement, religion, neighborhood, amount of privacy.[6] If one of these, such as education, shifts dramatically, class identity doesn't change.

Let me return to the statement of "fact" made by middle-class people: "You can't be working class. You have a university degree." I want to address this because I've heard it frequently, usually after I've asserted my working-class identity.

The remark contains arrogance that goes unnoticed by the speaker *(surprise, surprise)* but not by me *(surprise, surprise).* When a person with class privilege takes on the task of defining and articulating class location of someone from a lower class, it's arrogant and offensive.

Does this happen because working-class people claiming our identity threaten class-privileged people? In the United States, class is a taboo subject for everyone, let alone some upstart housecleaner or garbage man. Rich people need an automatic response, and seem to prefer a verbal attack that immediately silences the speaker. Discounting someone's identity usually does the trick.

This action is similar to the way white people try to shut me up when I critique racism: they question my identity as a person of color because of my light skin. Middle-class people attempt to shut me up by discrediting me, calling my identity into question, anything to stop me from claiming a working-class identity from which I might offer some criticism of their class privilege.

Implicit in middle-class people's assertion that I have indeed "moved up" is the ever popular belief that upward mobility is easily achieved and highly desirous. Neither of these is true, as far as I can tell. Some small percentage of working-class families have moved into the middle class in one or two generations, but they are the exception rather than the rule. As for upward mobility being highly desirable? Not for me. The values, ethics, simple lifestyles, and cultures of working-class people from any ra-cial/ethnic group appeal to me more than the constrained emotional life, isolation, and gross materialism of rich people. The only aspect of class privilege I find desirable is rich people's innate belief/knowledge that options about life—from job choice to education to creative activities—really do exist. Not to mention the freedom from despair over whether the rent will be paid or whether food will appear on the table.

how do you spell "class"?

Universities have changed in the last twenty years. Critiques of the system, hard questions, cross-disciplinary dialogues, new programs and departments springing up—Women's Studies, Ethnic Studies, Queer Studies. This is great, but what about class? I know the kind of rampant sexism, racism, and heterosexism progressive professors and administrators deal with as they struggle to change curricula, but it's hard to deal with the classism of this crowd because I expect more. I'm dismayed to read the advanced theories these people offer when discussing race, gender, or sexuality, and contrast that to blank looks about the c-l-a-s-s word.[7]

I've heard progressive professors present information about social change movements, and been excited to study common people's history and struggles. But I'm angry when pertinent information about participants' class location doesn't enter the discussion. In a lecture about the 1960s' Black civil rights movement, a professor carefully delineated racial issues but somehow forgot to mention that most people putting their asses on the line were poor. Another professor discussed "gay men" and "lesbians" fighting back at the Stonewall riots. I didn't learn until later that Black and Puerto Rican drag queens and white butches and femmes really carried off the honors; none of them held executive day jobs.[8] I want to call progressive professors on their failure to integrate class into the curriculum, on their failure to notice they are as out-to-lunch about class as the straight white men they criticize.

Hand in hand with changes to existing institutions, I propose the establishment of new institutions. I want Working Class Studies set up. I want working-class and working-poor histories, cultures, ideologies, theories, languages studied. I want the many worthy individuals who spent their lives working for social justice studied and examined. I want us teaching each other, want the labor halls and community centers filled with janitors, secretaries, housecleaners, garbage men, lineworkers, want us in charge of curriculum and reading lists and teaching. I envision us at the center; I don't want "experts" explaining our lives to us, standing behind a lectern and pontificating for two hours on proletarians.

Maybe I'm paranoid, but I anticipate this reaction to my idea: *You've got to be kidding.* Eyes focused on the front of the room, looking anywhere else but toward me, silence, shifting bodies, unease, a bright smile from the professor: "Thank you for that interesting suggestion. Shall we move on?" *It's happened to me before. Once I actually told a group of rich, white students I thought we should have Class Speak-Outs where only poor people could speak. No one looked at me. My words rolled into a hole in the middle of the floor and disappeared from the face of the earth.* I know what the reaction to this will be: what on earth are you suggesting? *Study a bunch of stupid rednecks?*[9] Chuckle, chuckle.

conclusion

At 3:00 p.m., construction workers on the University of Minnesota campus finish up. Privileged university students grumble about what an easy job these guys have and how early they're leaving. They have no idea these workers arrived at 6:00 or 7:00 in the morning. They don't know how a body feels after eight hours of physical labor. They don't care.

As for me, I just watch the workers go by and feel many things. I feel at home, because these men look so familiar, from their flannel shirts, jeans, and workboots down to lunch pails and thermoses, cigarettes, and hard hats. I feel comfortable, because I like being around them. *These are my people. And we're not stupid.* I feel angry, because I know how students and professors perceive these workers. Because I know some of these workers believe the lies about who's stupid and who's smart, who has the right to think and study here and who has the right to build and clean here.

But I am clear. *I'm working-class. I'm smart. Just like the people I grew up with.* We know how to screw the system, we know how to take care of ourselves and survive when the odds are against us. We cook tasty meals with one onion, build our own stereo speakers, cut precisely-fitting pieces of wood for porches, know how to wire our houses and sew clothes, we like to read and think and talk to each other. We make music and art and tell stories. We know how to work cooperatively and we know how to give, generously, both hands open.

I've figured out I belong in the university. Not just when they need a janitor, or a cook, or a construction worker. But when I want to go. If I choose to study there, I won't let anyone make me feel stupid; I'll remember why it's so important they try. I won't let them turn me into an assimilationist, a fraud, a middle-class-identified polite girl who's grateful for all the help these nice rich people offer. I'll stay true to my roots. I'll use my brains, and my hands, to take this system apart. I'll use my brains, and my hands, to get your feet off my neck.

notes

1. Thanks to Jan Binder, Elizabeth Clare, Cynthia Lane, Jeff Nygaard, and Susan Raffo for their help with this piece.
2. In this essay, when I use the word "rich," I mean anyone middle-class and up. Poor means anyone working-class and down. That is the way the working-class and working-poor people I grew up with use the terms. I find these categories problematic on one hand because they miss a lot of the subtleties of class. For example, they ignore my privilege of being working-class instead of working-poor. On the other hand, I still find them powerful and appropriate categories. Middle-class people, who could choose to realize they are also being duped by rich people and decide they would be better off aligning themselves with working-class and working-poor people, continually align themselves with the rich. This is another reason to include middle-class people in the "rich" group.
3. From *Webster's New Collegiate Dictionary*, 1979.
4. Thanks to Jeff Nygaard for helping me articulate this point.
5. I also know other working-class people who have earned a university degree and are no longer working-class identified. These people are intent on passing and assimilating. I'm not sure if they are really middle-class, but they are certainly middle-class identified.
6. Thanks to Dr. Katie Cannon, for articulating all of this so clearly.
7. A notable exception to the lack of discussion/curriculum around this issue are the courses I took from Dr. Katie Cannon, which consistently dealt with critical questions relating to race, class, sex, ability, and sexuality. Dr. Cannon is continuing this groundbreaking work at Temple University in Philadelphia.
8. I want to mention here the regular inclusion, in Women's Studies, of the women's campaign to get the vote. I believe it is an important struggle to study, but I've also come to believe that part of its popularity in women's studies is that the social location of those activists reflects the social location of the women teaching in those programs in a way that other struggles usually do not.
9. For the best discussion I have ever read on the offensiveness of rich people using the term "redneck," read Elliott, "Whenever I Tell You the Language We Use is a Class Issue, You Nod Your Head in Agreement—and Then You Open Your Mouth," *Out of the Class Closet: Lesbians Speak*, Julia Penelope, editor (Freedom, CA: The Crossing Press, 1994). Elliott's article first appeared in *Lesbian Ethics*, vol. 4, no. 2 (Spring 1991).

Halfbreeds

for my dog Grace

After your words of praise
for this wild canine,
I served details
while Grace crunched oak.
"Didn't know those two mixed."
At this wellworn refrain,
my mouth puckered,
I worked to hide it
while explaining
her unanticipated entry
into the world.

You scrutinized Grace,
then me, my
yellow skin
a perfect cross of
father's brown
and mother's white.
I stared back
at freckles
on collision course
with African features.

Our laughter bumped in mid-air,
Grace howled, we followed suit,
bent double,
careful of bottle shards
at our feet,
three accidents in close proximity.

In the dream
you both dashed
for the open field
leashes left behind
police in full pursuit.
I could not keep up
my bare feet soon bloody
on hot pavement.
I stood and watched
heart bursting,
they followed canine and human
diligently
forcefully
the chase extending
so far
I could not tell
which dark body
was thrown down to the ground
ground down
beaten to a pulp.

Dog, woman, man
all of us mutts
accidents.
"Didn't know those two mixed."
Visible reminders of
transgressive leaps
across social sanctions.
Too dark by half.

Catholic School Days

Lucy you know
the world must be flat
cuz when people leave town
they never come back.

*T*hese words of country singer Hal Ketchum's "Small Town Saturday Night" scratch a little at my heart every time I hear them. He's singing about fleeing small towns but I hear more. I remember girls falling off the face of the earth and never coming back. Pregnant girls, to be specific. Through Grades 7, 8, and 9, pregnant girls dropped off the face of a flat and uncaring earth with reckless abandon. No one batted an eye.[1]

Although Suzanne Beaulieu had two years on me, we spent Grades 6, 7, and 8 together because she failed twice. Not because she was stupid. Flunking connected to poverty, not brains. Suzanne didn't seem to care about failing or about our regimented daily routine. She blatantly disobeyed rules and laughed, frequently, at nuns, priests, her family, boys who flocked around her. Suzanne had the throatiest, most inviting laugh I've ever heard. Decades later I can still hear it. She'd smile and chuckle a few times, then throw back her head, leaving her mouth wide open, and gurgle infectiously.

The day Sister Mary Joseph made an oblique reference to the dangers of short skirts, Suzanne promptly crossed her legs and hiked up her miniskirt a few more inches, smiling broadly the whole time. The day Sister Ann Richard hauled Suzanne in after catching her smoking behind the portables, Suzanne acted out the scolding in great detail, including a fabulous imitation of Sister Ann's whine. No one laughed harder than Suzanne at the conclusion of her tale.

Suzanne and me, two halfbreed girls, Native and white, Arab and white, working-class, brains but no escape plans. They offered us a few choices that overall didn't amount to much but we made the most of them; I tried to hide in baggy green sweatpants and North Star running shoes, while Suzanne showed up at the other end of the continuum in a short, tight red skirt, tight red-checked polyester blouse, and flat red pumps.

I still see working-class girls these days who look like Suzanne—thick makeup, short skirts, buttons undone to show whatever cleavage that might or might not be there. "Bad" girls, according to middle- and upper-class norms, but all I see are survivors with brains working furiously and sweetness struggling to keep itself intact against the world's hard edges. And I remember Suzanne, just before she dropped off the face of the earth at the ripe old age of fourteen.

Let me attempt to write down only the facts, and ignore the knots of cold rage snaking in the pit of my stomach. We hit menstruation, and pregnancy jumped from girl to girl as easily as a cold. The only immunity seemed to be a father who worked in the office at general motors instead of on the line. But Suzanne, Kathy, Elizabeth, Wendy, Laurie, Beverly, Maria, Theresa, and me didn't have that immunity. We all got pregnant.

I got pregnant the way survivors of child sexual abuse usually get pregnant: rape. I don't know which of my many perpetrators was responsible for this pregnancy, and in any case, that's not important. I do know I couldn't be the only survivor in this group. Kathy, Theresa, and Wendy never dated boys, but somehow got pregnant. Suzanne had a boyfriend whose daring act was putting his tongue inside her mouth when they kissed.

How did so many of us get pregnant? I believe that most of us were raped by adult men, some girls got coerced into sex by boys our age, and one or two actually consented to—and possibly enjoyed—sex with a boyfriend. Of course, no one talked about any of this. No one talked about menstruation, fathers who visited in the night, priests who pried girls open on the altar, expectant girls without boyfriends. One of the many insidious forms of violence at our catholic school was enforced silence, and the locks circling our throats were every bit as brutal as rapes and assaults. I believe every girl in the school could have disappeared and no one would have said a word. Sex education during Sister Mary Joseph's health class? Not a chance. Concern for girl after girl dropping off the face of the earth? Only sealed lips. Encouragement for girls to talk about the reality of our daily lives? The world would have ended before that happened.

My parents thought the sun set and rose with the catholic church, and unquestioningly believed all doctrine, including the church's anti-abortion stand. My mother wore a particularly disgusting brooch shaped like a pair of baby's feet, known as "The Blessed Feet," to indicate her support for the church's stand on abortion. Nevertheless, my parents arranged for my abortion and dropped me off at the hospital themselves. While this may seem hypocritical, such a small example hardly begins to match the high standards for hypocrisy set by the catholic church.

My parents did not take me for an abortion because of concern for my well-being, or because I wanted one. They didn't consult me, and they didn't care about my well-being or my desires. My guess is that they took me for an abortion because of my mother's burning desire and futile effort to move into the middle class. In middle-class families—which to me meant Protestant—drinking, raping, battering, and swearing took place behind heavy, closed doors. Girls got pregnant just as often as they did in our families. The difference? Middle-class girls got abortions.

Back then, I understood none of this. After my beating I was so far gone I didn't know my name. When my father beat me there were two possibilities. The first and most common involved a few slaps and direct punches, with a kick or two. These assaults meant nothing to me because I had turned my yellow skin into armor. I practiced by pouring boiling water on myself and touching red-hot irons to my skin. I could do these things without blinking an eye or changing my breathing. But my armor buckled when my father beat me up the other way, and that is what he did when my mother told him about my pregnancy. He was enraged because now he couldn't set up my abortion as he had the previous one—secretly, in the basement, with himself and his priest cronies tying me down and performing the procedure with only the benefit of knives. No anaesthetic necessary.

Furious over this missed opportunity, my father lit into me, and I did not expect to survive. Crumpled on the floor, feeling welts on my body from the black leather belt and internal spasming from the tips of hard black leather shoes and cement in my head from repeated and pulverizing contact with wall and floor, I focused on my breathing. *In and out, in and out. Very little stands between a body breathing and a body not breathing. Very little, and it's shrinking all the time. Very little, and right now there's not much of a divide. In and out, in and out.*

I don't know whether Suzanne spent her nights at home lying on a sparkling clean linoleum floor trying to stay alive. She never came to school with visible bruises, but most child abusers don't mark the face. Suzanne had a pretty face and skin with a brown tinge. Big brown eyes and a wide mouth, which she applied bright lipstick to with a reckless hand. She was generous to a fault, and always shared her lunch and whatever she shoplifted. One spring she spent every recess with girls two grades behind us who didn't know how to skip Double Dutch or Dolly Dutch. No small feat on her part, during those years when separation by grades loomed large and important. Patient, encouraging, she explained the process, demonstrated over and over, and held the rope ends forever and a day. Squeezing the younger ones by their scrawny shoulders, she urged them on to new skipping heights.

In spite of her generosity, her laughter, her brains, Suzanne Beaulieu did what so many girls before her did, and what so many who came after would do. She fell off the face of the earth. I felt nothing as I watched my friend fall, because feelings are a luxury when survival is at stake. I felt nothing, because I had to concentrate on breathing in and out, in and out, and if I'd grieved I would have lost my focus, and very little stands between a body breathing and a body not breathing.

I watched Suzanne and Kathy and Elizabeth and Wendy and Laurie and Beverly and Maria and Theresa fall off the face of the earth. At some fundamental level I knew this happened to us not because of yellow or brown or white skin but because we were female and catholic and our fathers worked the line. I watched, again and again and again, as people stubbed out cigarettes with more care than any one of us ever got.

Today, my understanding is more concrete. We experienced class oppression and gender oppression as specifically influenced and sanctioned by the catholic church in a general motors town. The church spelled out in no uncertain terms whose lives mattered and whose did not. Working-class catholic girls stood almost at the back of the line. Poor girls came after us.

And so, from a young age, I learned focusing on breathing is important. I learned the lives of me and Suzanne and the others would be dismissed with an attitude past the point of cavalier. I learned we were so useless and worthless, every one of us could have fallen off the face of the earth and no one would have batted an eye.

I see a man approaching our Grade 8 homeroom. His face and body are blurred, and I can't tell if he's an executive, a lineworker, a priest, a doctor. He carefully stubs out his cigarette before surveying my classroom. He frowns a little as he notices how few girls sit at their desks. And then he shrugs as he realizes nothing important is missing, and turns to continue on his way.

notes

1. Thanks to Jan Binder, Juliana Peques, and Susan Raffo for their help with this.

Making Sense of My Happy Childhood/ Creating Theory

*T*he hot room held eighty bored bodies waiting for fifty minutes to tick by. Our white male professor pompously read his only lecture concerning people of color: "The Family and Race." Up until this day, we had fulfilled our sociology requirement by listening to his sexist, heterosexist, and classist views on "the family."

Professor Clark stressed that Black people (other people of color not existing) place incredible emphasis on the family because of what they experience outside of it, a view I later found many people of color actually do hold dear. "Because of the racial harassment and prejudice that can plague these people in day-to-day life," he intoned solemnly, "they must have a safe refuge, a haven, where they can return at the end of the day."

I looked around my corner of the room at one South Asian woman, two Black men, and one Latina. Had any of them found a safe haven?

My home life didn't resemble those of the happy TV families I watched faithfully, and I never got that warm, fuzzy feeling kids supposedly have when remembering their childhood home. Instead, a familiar and ongoing terror literally froze up my joints whenever I thought about our small house on that corner lot. I was subjected to an unrelenting combination of severe physical abuse, gross neglect, assaultive emotional and psychological imprinting, and sexual abuse that began after birth and did not let up until I moved away at age nineteen. My father, the main perpetrator of my abuse at home, belonged to a group of catholic laymen and priests who regularly ritually abused/tortured[1] me.

Taking these experiences and theorizing about them is fraught with difficulties. First, there are emotions. I've only been able to theorize about this abuse after doing a lot of healing. At earlier stages in this work, I felt too much pain to think concretely about what happened and what it meant. Only recently have I been able to set my abuse history in a more analytical, reflective framework. Which doesn't mean leaving my feelings behind, or thinking "objectively" about these issues. For me, that's not possible or desirable.

Second, there's the world of theory itself. Creating theory is loaded with questions, complexity, and issues of political power. Who creates theory, whose theory gets validated, whose language is spoken, who benefits? Where child sexual abuse is concerned, tension exists between some therapists and psychiatrists who consider themselves experts on our lives, and politicized survivors who insist we must analyze and make sense of these experiences ourselves. I'm uninterested in theory from self-proclaimed experts who have no sense of the political context in which families exist, who make sweeping generalizations about the monolithic group of child sexual abuse survivors. At the same time, I don't believe only survivors can create theory, or that theory must be identity-based.

I'm open to theory from politically aware, emotionally supportive allies who perceive the relationship between themselves and survivors as one of equal partners with different life experiences. I'm also open to survivors tackling issues that didn't directly affect them—for example, a white survivor offering perspectives on intersections between racism and child sexual abuse. My own theory, illustrated in this essay, springs not only from personal experience but from attempts to support oppressed groups I don't belong to.

sexual abuse of children

From infancy and into adulthood, I experienced ongoing sexual abuse at the hands of my father, several white working-class men, several white middle-class men, and two upper-middle-class white priests. Covert and overt attempts to get help failed, and I did what many victims do in order to survive. I repressed memories of these assaults. Freud documented this practice in his work; when children experience severe trauma but no one believes or validates what happened, they submerge the memories into the subconscious mind. If/when they reach a point in their lives when it's safe to remember, they will.

My memories surfaced after my discovery of feminism gave me the strength to leave an abusive marriage and find a therapist to help me deal with that trauma. It shocked me—but not my therapist, as she informed me later—to find myself swamped with childhood memories of brutal assaults. For the next several years, I experienced the aftereffects of my childhood. I struggled with deep depression, frequent self-mutilation, a desperation to commit suicide, anxiety attacks that lasted for days on end, pain so intense I had trouble breathing, and terror that immobilized me.

I couldn't think clearly about my experiences, but avidly read other people's words in hopes they would help. Available feminist literature proved a lifeline against alienation and craziness. Theory about child sexual abuse as misogyny made sense to me. I still felt terrified of men, anxious to please, and unable to trust. Adult experiences only supported these feelings. Male violence against women was as common as green grass in the spring, especially for the married women I knew.

Alone among social activists, feminists have named this issue, documented survivors' stories, broken social silence, formed a movement, affected legal change, provided resources and services for survivors, and written theory. Finding a social-change movement that validated my experiences, and offered resources for healing, drew me into feminist organizing. I spent several years as an activist working to end violence against women. I became familiar with basic feminist theory that named rape, wife-battering, child sexual abuse, incest, and sexual harassment as manifestations of sexism and misogyny. According to this theory, when child sexual abuse occurs, male perpetrators commit acts on female victims that damage us, teach us about misogyny, and prepare us for a lifetime of serving men sexually and emotionally. This made sense to me, and placed my feelings about being female in a political context. I had always hated and been ashamed of my female body, so easily pried open, so easily ripped to shreds. I never felt good about being a woman, although I didn't want to be a man. I didn't want a specific gender as much as I wanted to be invisible, or rather, I wanted to be invisible to my perpetrators and visible to whoever might rescue me, although I doubted such a person existed. I didn't want anyone to perceive me as a possible sexual partner, and believed the fewer people who noticed me, the better.

I pushed on with my healing, and in my thirties reached a place where I could think clearly about my childhood. I had already begun working toward an integrated analysis of various oppressions, and understood the limitations and unhelpful, unethical nature of theories examining only sexism or racism or imperialism. Could I transfer this to child abuse? Could I examine child abuse without preconceived notions?

This essay is my first written attempt at such thinking. I've decided to focus on one type of abuse—child sexual abuse—because concretely analyzing all types of child abuse (psychological, physical, emotional, ritual, sexual) in one essay poses difficulties. While different forms often interconnect and overlap, I need to start by taking each form apart and examining it. Somewhere down the road, I'll juxtapose these in a larger context of interwoven abuse experiences.

I define child sexual abuse as an institutionalized structure encompassing different kinds of behavior that violates children. These include assaultive sexual actions ranging from inappropriate touching to anal/vaginal/oral rape, as well as child pornography and prostitution, voyeurism, and sexual harassment.

The trauma of child sexual abuse profoundly affects survivors in physical, sexual, emotional, psychological, spiritual, and political ways. Although often carried out against an individual, child sexual abuse is political as well as personal, and I'm focusing here on the social, collective meanings of abuse. Child sexual abuse teaches us lessons about power—who has it and who doesn't. These lessons, experienced on a bodily level, transfer into the deepest levels of our conscious and subconscious being, and correspond with other oppressive systems. Widespread child sexual abuse supports a racist, sexist, classist, and ableist society that attempts to train citizens into docility and unthinking acceptance of whatever the government and big business deem fit to hand out.

Age difference and power differentials between adults and children create a compelling beginning point in my examination of child sexual abuse. Children my own age didn't have the power to devastate me, adults did.[2] When I think back on my experiences, I recall that difference in social location—their adult status, my child status—jumped out at me early on. So did other variables, most notably gender, race, and class. In my adult life, as I listened to heartbreaking story after heartbreaking story from other survivors,[3] these differences popped up again. I heard stories of boys sexually abused by men, disabled girls sexually abused by able-bodied men, girls and boys sexually abused by women, girls of color sexually abused by white adults, working-class and working-poor children sexually abused by class-privileged adults.

Consider this scenario: an adult orally rapes a child. Do you think of an adult man raping a girl child? Are they of the same race and class? Which race and class? Are both able-bodied? I left the gender/class/race/ability of child and adult unspecified to show the many possibilities for filling in the blanks. While many people envision an able-bodied man and an able-bodied girl with similar race and class backgrounds, that limiting and limited understanding doesn't match my own experiences and the other survivors' stories that allow me to frame an understanding of the collective meaning of child sexual abuse. I have come to set child sexual abuse in a wider theoretical context as a phenomenon that stamps cultural lessons of power and dominance onto the bodies and minds of children.

Child sexual abuse teaches children about social/cultural hierarchies in ways that ensure we'll remember the gist of it (if not the details). Stamping information on bodies and imprinting it into body memory guarantees a high retention rate. This information necessarily covers more than sexism, since sexism isn't the sole source of oppression; racism, classism, ableism, and the systematic oppression of children also figure into these lessons.

When a working-class man of color rapes a working-class girl of color, he uses her body as a slate for teaching about the power of sexism and adulthood. When a middle-class white man rapes that same girl, he imprints cultural hierarchies of classism, racism, adulthood, and sexism on her body. When a white woman rapes a girl of color, she teaches the girl that whiteness and adulthood equal power. When a white, middle-class man rapes a disabled, white, middle-class boy, he informs the boy that power belongs to able-bodied adults.

Isn't abuse in which racism, classism, and/or ableism play a part rare? Doesn't most abuse occur between male perpetrators and female victims? I've been asked these questions by people who disagree with my theory. Maybe a few cases of white men raping girls of color fall under the category of "statistically insignificant," an academic phrase designed to silence particular victims. Certain incidences of abuse cause feminists[4] problems. For example, feminist theorists have generally not known how to handle stories of physical battering or sexual abuse by women. One writer called female-perpetrated incest "rare...(and) less serious and traumatic than incestuous abuse by male perpetrators."[5] Another suggested that apolitical women resist male domination by taking it out on the children—a euphemism for child abuse.[6] Both statements trivialize the experiences of girls and boys abused by women, and further traumatize survivors. They also indicate a reluctance to deal with abuse that can't be explained by sexism.

I'm not trying to argue on the basis of statistical findings but to push beyond current static and incomplete understandings of child sexual abuse. Suppose thirty years ago members of a liberation movement for people of color shared stories about surviving childhood rape by white adults. Suppose that helped more men and women of color to remember and/or break silence around experiences of child sexual abuse by white adults. What would theory about child sexual abuse look like now? How would we expand such theory and move it forward? Even if the majority of child sexual abuse cases occur between an adult male and a female child of the same racial background, it's necessary, important, and ethical to devise theory that adequately addresses a wide range of experiences in which various oppressions present themselves.

In examining various oppressions, I don't want to ignore one type of oppression present in almost every instance of child sexual abuse—that is, adults' power over children. This directly connects to the oppression of children, a phenomenon ignored and unnoticed by most people. In this society, children are regularly ostracized, trivialized, and minimized. Frequently denied the right to have input in decisions that directly affect their lives, they can't engage in even the smallest acts of self-determination. In custody battles, many kids can't even state their preferences about which parent they want to live with; in school, they have little or no voice in their educational process. This oppression has been in place so long that few people notice the systematic way children's desires and realities are not only ignored but consistently denied.

There are other insidious examples of child oppression. Basic needs for food and shelter go unmet.[7] Staggering numbers of children experience physical, sexual, emotional, psychological, and ritual abuse. Good childcare and positive educational experiences are rare; in the current posturing about balancing the federal budget, money is constantly cut from one institution that specifically serves children—the school. The current phenomenon euphemistically called "welfare reform" constitutes a direct attack on poor children, who have no direct voice in the governmental bodies enacting such "reform." Then we have the right-wing push for "family values." A pretense of concern for families covers an agenda guaranteed to devastate children: keep them at home with abusive parents; make divorce difficult no matter how much battering a woman and her children experience; prevent queer couples from raising children. Last but not least is the terrifying increase in children who are drugged. The prescription of Ritalin for any child diagnosed as hyperactive, and anti-depressants for any child exhibiting symptoms of depression (which match the signs for abuse), has risen dramatically over the past couple of years. Instead of listening to kids, or checking for clues about home or social life, many psychiatrists, therapists, and parents seem happy to keep them stifled with drugs.

These examples of systematic oppression cannot be reduced to personalized, individualized, disconnected events. The oppression of children must be routinely woven into our theory, along with sexism, racism, classism, imperialism and ableism, and theory about child sexual abuse must contain *all* these elements.

In pushing for an understanding of child oppression, I'm not urging the pendulum to swing into the direction of the spoiled brat. That's just the flip side of the kid who's given no say. I'm looking for parents to set healthy, respectful boundaries, to allow the movement toward self-determination and thoughtful decision-making to correspond to a child's development. Rules aren't helpful here because each child is different, and of course cultural definitions of what constitutes a child and how to treat one vary wildly. While I'm aware of these complexities, I still believe all children have a basic right to food, shelter, clothes, education, respect, and freedom from abuse.

I also believe the systematic nature of child oppression impresses upon children that their desires, feelings, thoughts, and experiences don't matter. This early training sets the stage for adult life, in which this cavalier disregard for personal, family, and social suffering gets passed down through generations.

connecting child sexual abuse to other oppressions

One of my goals in this essay is to connect child sexual abuse and other forms of oppression. First, I want to document how the institutions of racism, classism, and ableism get played out in child sexual abuse. I believe child sexual abuse supports and reinforces these institutions, and thus serves the status quo.

racism

Child sexual abuse severely damaged my racial identity as Arab. A set of culturally specific, oppressive stereotypes around sex is attached to each community of color. Within these stereotypes, Arab men appear as beastly, animal-like, hairy brutes who will fuck anything that moves and who love being cruel. Arab women, like other Asian women, are painted as docile, exotic, anxious to serve men sexually, and filled with secret knowledge of exciting positions and actions. Once "opened up" by the right man (usually the white man), the Arab woman turns into a sex-crazed, sex-hungry "slut" who will beg for it all night long.

I didn't experience these oppressive stereotypes theoretically or abstractly. The white men who abused me continually brought these ideas to the fore through verbal comments made before, during, and after their sexual assaults. They referred to my Arab features, remarked on my skin color, told me Lebanese girls enjoyed it, forced me to "belly dance," and repeatedly threw epithets such as "Arab slut" at me.

Wider society had taught me—albeit not at such close quarters—that my Arab identity was suspect and shameful. These intimate assaults reinforced that. I hated being Arab; I wanted to turn my yellow skin inside out, to bleach my whole skin with the burning chemicals I applied to the hair on my upper lip, to assimilate without a backward glance. I can't imagine any Arab girl holding onto pride in her cultural background in the face of similar ongoing assaults. I did not.

My father's attacks further damaged my racial identity. First, he fit the stereotype of Arab men so well it caused me further shame, this time by association. Second, he broadcast his contempt for anything Arab through his abuse of me, a contempt arising in part from hatred of self.

I despised my father, in part because he played into racist stereotypes, in part because he hated women and children. And yet I was linked to him through blood *and* race. This connection caused me to further internalize racism.

classism

Intelligent depictions of working-class reality appear on the silver screen once in a blue moon. So I almost fell out of my seat at *Loyalties*, a film that critically examines child sexual abuse, race, class, domestic violence, heterosexual relationships, and friendship. I highly recommend it. That most Americans don't know about this amazing Canadian film angers but doesn't surprise me.

In the movie, an upper-middle-class white male physician plans to rape the Native, working-class daughter of the woman who cleans his house. While painful to watch, *Loyalties* proved a healing experience for me, because it clearly shows how class privilege connects with child sexual abuse. In order to abuse, an abuser needs access. The physician had access to the young girl partly because of his class location, just as the girl's father, a working-class Native man, had little access to the doctor's children, partly because of class location.

Access constitutes a central tenet of class privilege. Capitalism relies on rich people having uninterrupted access to poor people's bodies. Otherwise, how would work get done? And rich people can't rest after only securing access to our labor. They claim it all: dominance over every part of us, including our sexuality. Working-class women in factories experience routine harassment and sexual violation by men in positions of power, from foremen to executives. In these settings, class privilege counts every bit as much as male privilege.

Through child sexual abuse I learned about access—who has it, who doesn't. Many men gained entrance to my body, but not all men. None "beneath" my family, which included poor men, were granted this opportunity. But for men equal and above it was open season. Executives, teachers, and priests claimed access, demanded it in vicious ways. My feelings and thoughts remained inconsequential, as inconsequential as those of factory workers who don't enjoy inhaling thick smoke and standing in filth all day long.

As a child, I learned my class identity marked me and put me at high risk, and came to believe girls from privileged families had more protection. After all, if no one beneath my family could get to me, the same must hold true for them. Since fewer men lived at or above their class level, they must be safer. Class identity protected them; mine endangered me.

In spelling out what I believed as a child, which originated in large part from the multiple assaults I experienced, I'm not saying class privilege prevents child sexual abuse. Plenty of middle-class and upper-class perpetrators violate their children.[8]

ableism

My understanding of this strand of oppression differs from the previous two; it doesn't emerge directly from personal experience, but rather from being an ally to disabled people. While it feels presumptuous to create theory based on someone else's experiences, particularly when able-bodied people like to present ourselves as saviors to the "poor unfortunates," it feels more irresponsible to ignore the issue or mention it only in passing.[9]

The term "bodily integrity" is used by disabled activists and/or survivors of child abuse to indicate a state of being in which a person controls her own body and who has access to it. Violation of bodily integrity is a trusted tool for keeping ableism's machinery running smoothly, and it often comes about through the "help" of able-bodied people. Articulating this doesn't deny or ignore the fact that some disabled people need assistance completing certain tasks. Neutral, casual, no-strings-attached assistance is one thing. I'm talking about help distinguished by lack of control on the part of disabled people, reinforcement of social power dynamics between able-bodied and disabled people, literal, physical handling of a person without consent or in spite of objections. While most disabled people communicate how, why, when, and where they want touch from able-bodied people, the latter group continually ignores this and tugs, prods, pulls, pushes, carries, turns, moves, or lifts after having made a decision for the disabled person. The medical system offers a stalwart example of painful hands-on touch and constant denial of bodily physical reality ("No, this doesn't hurt.").

Suppose child sexual abuse enters this picture—which it does with astounding frequency in residential schools and homes, psych wards, nursing homes, family dwellings, and "caregiving" facilities. Through talking with and reading the works of politicized disabled people, I've learned child sexual abuse runs rampant in these institutions and happens more often than not. From doctors to caregivers, from nurses' assistants to staff workers and parents, disabled children remain at appalling risk.

A disabled child undergoing sexual abuse experiences something already well known—lack of control over her/his own body. In eerily-familiar ways, able-bodied adult abusers violate children's space, and teach them that they can't control how, when, or why touch happens. Once again, child sexual abuse reinforces lessons about powerful social institutions and how they work. Various kinds of physically intrusive contact—ranging from rape to having food shoved down your throat when you're not hungry—drive home the ableist message that disabled people's bodies are fair game for the rest of us.

docile citizens

In the previous sections I examined the ways children learn about particular systems of oppression through child sexual abuse, how in its most general sense child sexual abuse serves the status quo. Now I want to continue looking at the same thing, but from a different angle, more of a macro level than a micro level. What happens in an oppressive society when a large proportion of people are sexually abused during childhood? What kinds of repercussions does this have for society at large? Does it support the status quo? If so, how? How does child sexual abuse affect all survivors—regardless of our race, class, or ability?

Child sexual abuse is a horrible thing. And it's not just the isolated attacks, the rapes and violations, that make it so horrible. Rape is horrible. No question. *And* the system surrounding it is equally insidious, in some ways more insidious than the rapes themselves. Let me spell this out. I grew up surrounded by perpetrators who smiled in public and destroyed in private. I learned I was an object to be used, that no one respected my body, my personhood, my subjectivity. I experienced severe pain that seemed to me obvious, but no one responded. The world didn't give a damn. I grew up believing the world is a crappy place, always expected the worst, and always assumed no one cared. After all, that was my reality. As an adult, when confronted with any new realizations about just how crappy the world really is—clearly perceiving the racist, imperialist, heterosexist structures surrounding me—I wasn't surprised. My deepest beliefs from childhood were simply confirmed. When I learned about these issues, when activists urged me to talk, become educated, organize, fight back, resist, I felt terror about doing so. My instinct, pounded into me physically and psychologically from a young age, was to keep silent and not confront anyone.

Child sexual abuse happens at a time when vulnerable children are developing a sense of self and a sense of the world, when we're developing connections and relationships with other people, when we're discovering how the world works and what we can expect from it. The beliefs, ideas, and attitudes that root during these years take us through our lives. (In pointing this out, I'm not saying these beliefs, ideas, and attitudes can't be changed.)

Let me spell out the structural aspects of child sexual abuse I grew up with. First, the secretive nature. Obviously, it's not openly acknowledged. No one said a word about this incredibly important aspect of my life. I knew it was happening. But perpetrators, their accomplices, and society at large told me it wasn't. They told me I was lucky to be surrounded by such good christian men. I learned about denial, about people refusing to acknowledge what literally stared them in the face, about injustice and oppression as secrets that can't be talked about. Sound familiar? Remind anyone of the blank stares on the faces of people being told about atrocities and massacres, about environmental pollution, about violence against women?

The secrecy and denial are closely linked with silence. Survivors keeping silent is of vital importance to perpetrators. Yet most of us manage to speak about it, directly or indirectly. I was no exception. From covert appeals to aunts, teachers, and family friends, to sitting down with my grade school principal and spelling out what the priests did to me, I attempted to break through the web of insidious silence. The result? Ignored and disbelieved, beaten to the point of death, locked up in a psych ward.

I learned firsthand about political oppression *and* about the denial, secrecy, silence, and brutal repercussions that go hand in hand with it. Injustice exists, yes, but don't name it and don't fight it. If no one cared about what happened to me as a child, in a society where people supposedly love children, why would anyone care about Palestinians in the West Bank? Why would political organizing appeal to me? Why would I assume I could take on a group of corporate executives who want to use my neighborhood as a toxic waste dump, when, after I put up one hand in a rather feeble attempt to stop one large adult male rapist, he banged my head on a wall for several long minutes?

After all, I already know what corporate executives are likely to do. People with power use it in horrible ways: they violate you however they want and they get away with anything. No one stops them, no matter how blatantly they flaunt their actions. Why would I tangle with a group of these people? Why would I want to take them on? And even if I did, what effect would it have? Resistance is futile. Remember?

Resistance is futile, no matter how much pain and suffering is going on all around you. I grew up in extreme pain and suffering. Looking back, the signs were obvious. Bruises all over me, catatonic state, consistently bloody underwear, constant anxiety and fear, inability to sleep. Not to mention talking openly about it. But my pain and suffering meant nothing. No one cared. There are important repercussions here. If I spend the first twenty years of life realizing no one cares about my pain, can I care about anyone else's? What chance is there that I can get to a genuine and generous place of healthy compassion? How willing will I be to take on the system?

I truly believe the powers that be want a society filled with docile, unthinking citizens who won't resist, challenge, and organize to change the many insidious forms of oppression around us. Many factors work into this, including the effects of such things as drugs, poverty, and television. But it's important that people not ignore the ways child sexual abuse supports the deadly status quo.

Thousands of survivors numbed out from pain, denial, and silence don't make good activists. Repression of memories intensifies the numbness, and huge numbers of survivors do push down memories of the actual abuse. It's worth noting that repressing memories of detailed incidents of abuse doesn't mean forgetting the lessons about life the abuse teaches. Survivors don't forget knowledge of powerlessness, of denial and secrecy and support for oppression. Memory repression doesn't block out those lessons, but it does take an enormous effort. It's energy draining, and it stops people from becoming psychologically or emotionally healthy. How could anyone be healthy with chunks of life missing from his or her own memory, with profound, life-shaping experiences unavailable to the conscious mind?

I engaged in some political organizing work before I remembered and dealt with my childhood experiences. I wasn't able to interact well or challenge problematic abuses of power and privilege in these groups. Not surprisingly, chances for healthy group interaction, thoughtful reflection, and meaningful actions were limited. Most political activists have watched groups fall apart because of horrible group dynamics. As I've watched this happen in recent years, I've had strong hunches that unresolved childhood trauma was at least partly responsible for what happened.

To change the world, we need engaged, emotionally healthy people. This doesn't mean we hide out for decades in a therapist's office before venturing to show up at a demo. It does mean we understand that our most deeply set beliefs and ideas profoundly affect our organizing work, that our childhood experiences, ranging from dysfunction to extreme abuse, need to be tackled in the same way oppressive social systems need to be tackled.[10]

the left

Outside of feminism, progressive movements rarely state opposition to child abuse, let alone take action. I can't conceive of any acceptable reasons for this great failure. I certainly don't buy the response that men fighting racism would weaken their focus by including child abuse. Acknowledging and analyzing child abuse—as well as sexism, heterosexism, classism, ableism—strengthens our ability to analyze and resist racism.

When we take a step back and figure out who's organized against child sexual abuse and why, several things become clear. Feminists have tackled the issue and come up with an analysis of child sexual abuse stemming largely from gender oppression and sexism. In other words, a safe analysis for a group predominantly made up of women. This analysis draws a safe boundary around the people out "there" (that is, men) who abuse children, and the people "here" who don't. No wonder survivors bringing up issues of abusive mothers didn't go over so well in the women's movement.

For social-change movements to take seriously what I'm saying about child sexual abuse (and I'm including feminists here), activists must acknowledge the bad people who rape children are not out there, they're in here. We know this from survivors' stories; perpetrators come from every place in the political spectrum. The lines can't be clearly drawn anymore. All of us have to seriously grapple with the fact that perpetrators regularly attend our meetings and our demos.

While I do not ignore the genuine concern feminists have for child abuse, it seems clear to me feminists began the discussion because it was safe to do so. No group members were challenged. Now it's time to move on. If we're going to change the situation, we need to start with strong, mature political activists who aren't afraid to acknowledge that there are perpetrators in our groups.

Dealing with child abuse involves several things for activists. First, we need the maturity and strength to take stock of misuses of power and privilege within our groups. Second, we need to follow through with what we say; if we truly do care about all oppressed peoples, we must extend this to kids down the street. Third, we must engage in clear strategic thinking about the ramifications of large-scale child abuse. The strength of left-wing movements comes in part from helping people engage in critical thinking, from helping people steer clear of unquestioningly accepting the falsehoods spewed out daily by the mass media. Child sexual abuse, as a phenomenon, directly benefits big business and government by ensuring a compliant population. As I outlined earlier, such childhoods don't steer us toward a life of street activism and critical thinking; rather, we end up with a fear of authority, a willingness to accept tyranny, a terror of fighting back.

Feminists have achieved extraordinary successes in spite of these factors by organizing against child abuse and empowering survivors. Many of us have learned to question authority, to refuse to accept abuse as a normal part of life, to fight back, and to analyze, reject, and counter misinformation not only about ourselves but about prisoners, the Two-Thirds World, homeless people. There's a message here for other progressive movements.

conclusion

Each day I'm disgusted by the lies about family, home, children, and parents that circulate in the media, schools, churches, and government—lies about warm feelings toward family dwellings, childhood as a time of innocence and happiness, parents' ever-present love for children, and fond memories of and nostalgic desires to return to tender years. As politically calculated as those about people of color and disabled people, these lies obscure reality and support abusers.

As political activists, we need to break through the lies, must listen to children and to adult survivors who tell the truth of life inside cramped apartments and three-story mansions. We need to grapple with the huge numbers of survivors walking among us and, probably more difficult, the huge numbers of perpetrators walking among us. This will not be an abstract task, since perpetrators run the political spectrum from right-wing fascists to left-wing radicals. Clearly, this issue needs to be taken up, and taken seriously, by all progressive movements. It can't be left to feminists, nor can it be acknowledged as a personal, individual problem survivors need to deal with at home.

We need to support each other. If child sexual abuse—and other forms of child abuse—were routinely acknowledged in more political circles as important and worth taking seriously, we'd be in better shape. As well as integrating an analysis of various forms of oppression into our political work, I believe we also need to integrate personal experiences (without letting them take over every discussion). While individual therapy and healing physical touch from friends and trained, ethical professionals may be tools survivors utilize on the road to healing, it's equally important to know that fellow activists care about the issue and care about us. This helps break down the messages that we mustn't talk about the issue and that we must carry the trauma alone. Our own childhood experiences, ranging from severe abuse to racism in the schoolyard, must be part of the discussions in left-wing communities. While I'm blessed to have this integration of the personal and political in my life, I know it's the exception rather than the rule.

As activists, we can offer support within our own circles and we can influence the kind of care available to survivors. We can push for politicized therapists who understand how child sexual abuse fits with other oppressions, and who offer affordable therapy for everyone. And when we're lobbying for national health care, we need to make sure emotional/psychological health care is included. Rich people's medical benefits include private therapy. Why shouldn't ours?

As activists, we need to place child oppression in our political context. We can't talk about child abuse without acknowledging and examining child oppression. Where are children's concerns, issues, voices in our groups? How do we treat children, in our political work, in our home lives, in our communities? If we don't abuse them, do we treat them with dignity and respect?

Finally, I want to say that healing from traumatic experiences is possible. Difficult and painful and exhausting, but possible and very much worth the struggle. It has taken years for me to come to this, to discard earlier beliefs about myself as a broken individual in an uncaring world. With a supportive community, with a political analysis, with time, love and caring, survivors of child sexual abuse are able to confront the past, work through and let go of unhelpful belief systems, and move on to emotionally-vibrant, politically-active and fulfilling lives.

notes

1. I find the phrase "ritual abuse/torture" the most appropriate for describing this kind of abuse. "Ritual abuse" on its own doesn't indicate that the most brutal forms of torture are involved, and "torture" on its own ignores the systematic and carefully planned aspects of this kind of abuse. Keeping the phrase together with the slash (/) indicates the deep, intrinsic connections I experienced between them. A helpful resource is Chrystine Oksana, *Safe Passage to Healing: A Guide for Survivors of Ritual Abuse* (New York: Harper Perennial Press, 1994).
2. Girls are raped by boys their own age. That is child sexual abuse perpetrated against girls by perpetrators who have power over them because of the institution of sexism. When a man rapes a girl, there are aspects of at least two social institutions—sexism plus the power that comes with adulthood.
3. I still feel shock about the numbers of survivors I know personally. One set of statistics, verified by the FBI, that bastion of feminist activity, states that one in four girls and one in seven boys will be sexually assaulted before the age of eighteen. Actual incidence is probably a lot higher than that.
4. I'm singling out feminists because they're the only group which has consistently dealt with this issue.
5. Diana Russell, *The Secret Trauma* (New York: Basic Books, 1986), p. 298.
6. Andrea Dworkin, "Violence Against Women: It Breaks the Heart, Also the Bones," *Letters from a War Zone* (New York: E.P. Dutton, 1989), p. 174.
7. Other oppressions connect with the issue of which children's material needs are met and which are not.
8. Thanks to Elizabeth Clare for helping me clarify my thoughts around classism and ableism.
9. It's difficult to talk about disabled children as a cohesive group since their experiences vary so widely. For example, a deaf child living at home with parents who know American Sign Language has a much different experience from a child without use of arms and legs in a chronic care facility. Of course, most able-bodied people don't notice these intense differences, and tend to see all disabled people as weak and helpless.
10. Jan Binder gave me a great deal of help with this section.

Coiled Tongues[1]

Which tender body
shall be carved up
served on a platter
to Monsignor tonight?
Male or female?
White, yellow or brown?

Wavering at rectory door
I watched my father's car
grow smaller.
Catholic obedience
always goes too far.

Before Monsignor devours flesh
he dresses it properly
manipulates each limb carefully.
Do clerks blanch
when selling garter belts
and black nylons
to fit 10-year-old bodies?
Are store managers
appreciative accomplices
who insist Monsignor
take generous discounts?

Mouth a final blessing.
"You Lebanese girls are so pretty."
His voice slimed over my ribs,
anchored in.
Some words cannot be exorcised,
even with flames.

Monsignor savors flesh more
when flavored with lies.
"Yes, I liked it."
I memorized the force
of white fingers
picking my bones clean.

Years later
I remember the children
whose eyes slid under the pew
whose tongues tangled
when Monsignor walked by.
The VanDerHagen girls
the Beneditto boys
the Lee children.
I envision priests
marking names in ledgers
systematically recording each feeding.

Years later
at a party
someone tells a "joke":
A newly-ordained priest
celebrates with
a lavish table.
"If this is poverty, Father,"
asks a guest,
who could have been me
who would have said it grimly
"If this is poverty, Father,
what does chastity look like?"

Times change.
Time changes.
Bony and bloody remains
on platters
metamorphize slowly,
gather force.

Now
when he poisons the room
with his presence
our eyes will rivet instead of slide
tongues coil instead of tangle.
"What does chastity look like?"

The man with the backward collar
will chew fingernail, grip chair tightly
as this new reality strikes full force:
No bodies here
for carving, serving, devouring.

Memories withstand long decades.
Sins cast long shadows.
Take heed.
Broken children coil long tongues.

notes

1. For any reader fortunate enough to be unaware of the catholic church hierarchy, monsignors are above priests and below bishops. The rectory is the house next to the church where priests and monsignors live.

Still Listenin to that Sentimental Twang

alling into the car seat, I fasten my seat belt, turn over the ignition, and drive off. My body aches from a morning of scrubbing, vacuuming, and lifting, and my fingers sting from the chemicals they've been drenched in. I arch my back in an attempt to remove the kinks, and reach for the radio.

The terse, flat voice of a white, working-class Minnesota man requests Aaron Tippin's "I Got It Honest" for the guys at the garage. The announcer asks, "You identify with this song, do you?" With the classic understatement I've heard all my life from working-class men, the mechanic says, "Yup," capturing layers of meaning in one syllable.

When Aaron Tippin's voice comes on, I crank the radio and sing along at the top of my lungs.

> I never had to hang my head in shame
> For puttin a price tag on my name
> Never turned my back on what I believed
> Or let my heart be ruled by greed
> 'Cause buddy if I didn't earn it I don't want it
> That way I can always say I got it honest.

My tiredness, irritation, and achiness ebbs away with the words. Some one is singing about my life.

Now you ain't looking at some dude that was born
with a silver spoon in his mouth
And I might seem like some kind of low life to that
high falutin crowd
But I'm plain spoken straight talkin and damn
proud of what I have accomplished
And some folks 'preciate that some don't but I
got it honest.

Country-western music[1] is a rich expression of working-class and working-poor culture in the United States, emerging from the rural deep South. It has close ties to Appalachian culture, which in turn connects to Scottish, Irish, and English ballads. This tradition documents the lives and tells the stories of factory workers, waitresses, truck drivers, and prostitutes. It articulates the struggles of working-class women and men, and celebrates our values and ethics. While primarily originating from white communities, it has influenced and been influenced by musical forms of working-class people of color such as blues and gospel.

I grew up listening to country music because my father liked it. Early on, I came to love the compelling lyrics, the frugal background music, the fiddles and banjoes, the sentimentality, and the nasal twang of working-class Americans from the deep South—the twangier and more nasal, the better. For me, the working-class form and content dissolved geographic and racial boundaries between the musicians and myself. As a child, I identified keenly with the music, and was especially moved by Hank Williams singing "I'm So Lonesome I Could Cry."

Yet, beginning in high school and continuing through my twenties and early thirties, middle-class and upper-middle-class people let me know, in no uncertain terms, that my feelings for country music were suspect and shameful. No one could possibly enjoy such a "lowbrow," "inferior," and "stupid" form of music. Yes, these are direct quotes. Lacking a political analysis of class developed enough to decipher these cryptic comments, I couldn't discern the real messages of class elitism. And I didn't realize how these messages reinforced internalized self-hatred and community hatred. I stopped listening to country music.

Every so often, through my years of marriage to a middle-class man and a social circle of middle-class people, I heard a country song re-defined and thus accepted by the middle-class as "folk music," such as "Put Me on a Train Back to Texas" and "Georgia on my Mind." Waves washed over me at such moments—of homesickness, loneliness, loss. But I was too confused, inarticulate, and alienated to understand any of this. The song came and went, the elusive moment vanished, and a year or two passed before I'd hear it again.

A friend had a similar experience when she showed up, full scholarship in hand, on a university campus. The first week of class, her dorm roommate laughed derisively when she tuned in the country station: "You can't be serious." My friend learned quickly enough, but couldn't quite forsake her people's music. And so, on nights when she found herself alone, she'd crouch over her radio, keep the volume low, and listen to Patsy and Hank and Reba. For the length of an evening lecture, her sense of loss would be assuaged.

I've tried to analyze the many disparaging comments I've heard over the years, some of which came from upper-middle-class and middle-class people, while some came from working-class people who did not grow up in the South. I believe the negative attitude toward country music originates in at least three places. One is the dangerous and deep division in the United States between North and South; since country music comes from the South, northerners (and others) believe it's inferior and must be despised. (I'm amazed and horrified at an astoundingly commonplace action in the United States, carried out by people from all places on the political spectrum: people assume a fake southern accent to indicate that the speaker is stupid.) The second reason country music is so despised is because of the general disdain and scorn for any cultural activities of working-class and working-poor people.[2] The third arises specifically from the rural roots of the music. In our society, the urban/rural split is an important social division, and anything or anyone rural is put down and trivialized. Class solidarity doesn't hold here; members of working-class urban communities routinely mock rural working-class communities.

As I see it, the working-class roots, southern location, and rural nature of country music overlap and connect to create a distorted view in many people's minds, drawing out three strong intolerances which are for the most part unexamined and deep. I've caught glimmers of this hatred coming through comments flung at me because I listen to country. Sometimes these attacks have been vicious. Perfect strangers—unasked—gave their opinion clearly and forcefully. I haven't experienced this with other music. Even when people don't like my choice of reggae, hard rock, or classical, they don't respond so viscerally and angrily.[3]

What are some of these comments so vehemently directed my way? And, perhaps more importantly, how do I make sense of them?[4]

1. "Three chords and lyrics an eight-year-old could write. You call that music?"

First, country music varies widely in terms of simplicity and difficulty, and it's impossible to make sweeping generalizations. Many song lyrics contain short, clear phrases that can be easily remembered. This format was particularly important in earlier times when the majority of listeners, who couldn't read or write, passed the songs down orally. Country music is derived in part from Scottish, Irish, and English ballads, which contain short phrases and much repetition,[5] and that tradition still influences today's music. Yet, blues, Cajun, and rock also contain easy-to-remember lyrics, and I don't hear these musical forms criticized as ridiculously simple.

Instrumentally and vocally, country music has space for beginning and advanced musicians. Elaborate vocal harmonizing and yodeling challenge singers. Beginners who only know the guitar chords of C, G, and D can play along, and other musical lines allow advanced banjo, fiddle, dobro, and guitar players to elaborate and solo. Beginning and advanced musicians can perform side by side, each at their own level, a characteristic vital to people who can't read or write music but play by ear. In the early days of country, few musicians read or wrote music.

Second, so what? Is artistic beauty and value based on complexity? Does cultural expression have to be difficult, incomprehensible, and inaccessible? In my book, it doesn't. Even in the books of Western, elitist art critics, it doesn't. But once again, the class location of the artist comes into play. This can be seen clearly when looking at particular forms of modern-art paintings. I stood in front of a huge canvas covered with brown paint in a prestigious Toronto gallery, and said, "I could do this." After all, what could be more simple? I've since discovered critics would consider this statement proof of my lack of sophistication. They've constructed meaning around these types of paintings that allows the art to be understood only by "experts" who have studied and studied, to be inaccessible and incomprehensible, at the same time that it is simple. The painting measures up to arbitrary standards controlled by the elite world of art criticism. On the other hand, country music, which is simple *and* accessible *and* comprehensible *and* (almost) anyone can create it, won't cut it with these critics.[6] Accessibility draws their scorn and stigmatizes the simplicity, and this attitude of scorn filters down through the culture. Thus people are able to tell me country music is no good.

2. *"This is really exciting. One song after another about being dumped."*

I'm quite fond of this comment, with all its elitist impatience. It reminds me of a joke I've heard many times: What do you get when you play country music backward? Your wife, your dog, your truck.

Now, this joke can be interpreted two different ways. As often happens with humor, it can solidify an oppressive viewpoint. In this example, it reinforces a problematic and narrow understanding of country music as a series of songs by redneck[7] losers whining about their troubles. Conversely, this joke also manages to address the deep losses working-class people routinely experience, and allows us to laugh about them. When I hear this joke, I laugh because it's funny and true *and* it touches on something profound that really isn't funny—in this instance, the loss that pervades working-class/working-poor lives.

So many country songs focus on the centrality of loss—of a lover, a job, a child, a way of life, a family farm, a piece of land, dignity, pride. Through the decades, a great many things have been taken from us. We've stood and watched as bankers repossessed homesteads; we've helped sons and daughters board the bus because the land could no longer sustain them; we've waved good-bye to family members as they left for work in the morning and then got the news about another "accident" in the mine; we've buried young children because we couldn't afford medical care; and we've watched plants close and towns die because a rich man thousands of miles away signed a piece of paper. These tremendous and yet everyday losses are recorded in our music. Iris DeMent illustrates this in her song "Our Town," about the death of a hometown and the displacement of a resident:

> Now I sit on the porch and watch the lightnin bugs fly
> But I can't see too good, I got tears in my eyes
> I'm leavin tomorrow but I don't wanna go
> I love you, my town, you'll always live in my soul
> But I can see the sun's settin fast
> And just like they say, nothing good ever lasts
> Go on, I gotta kiss you goodbye
> But I'll hold on to my lover 'cause my heart's bout to die
> Go on now and say goodbye to my town, to my town
> I can see the sun has gone down on my town, on my town
> Goodnight, Goodnight

Along with country songs documenting loss of jobs, land, innocence, and family are the country songs about messy triangles, heartaches, cheating, being dumped, and passionate betrayals. A large, very large, number of country songs locate these issues front and center. From many rich people, I've heard that there are just too many of these songs, a clear over-abundance, and their irritation fascinates me. I believe it's connected to the common classist belief that working-class/working-poor people are continually guilty of excess. We drink too much, we smoke too much, we laugh too loud, if we are femmy girls we wear too much makeup and our skirts are too short, if we are masculine boys we drive too fast and wear our muscle shirts too tight. Our love affairs are too sordid and too public. Even within our music, we are guilty of excess. A significant question arises from this upper-class critique of working-class excess: who's truly guilty of excess? Is there a little projection going on here? Pay no attention to the glutton behind the curtain whose standard of living is sucking the planet dry—look at how many thick gold chains, bought for a measly $10 each, the guy in the souped-up Chevy has around his neck, and damned if he isn't blasting one of those somebody-done-somebody-wrong songs from a tinny car stereo.[8]

So what if there are a lot of tragic love songs? I like them, for many reasons. Listening to them after being dumped helps me realize I'm not alone and lets me wallow as pathetically as I like. They offer another vehicle (this one metaphorical, the one I described with Iris DeMent's song being more literal) for recording our systemic losses. And they record reality, real life happenings. People get dumped all the time. People fall in love with the wrong person all the time. People have sordid affairs all the time. And I don't mean just poor people. I can verify that these things also happen to rich people, having cleaned their houses for years.

Another musical form that deals with sorry tales of love as intensely as country is the blues, which has also been ridiculed as a simple set of "life done me wrong" songs. I want to take a look at what's happened with the blues, and the way members of the dominant elite respond to the blues (an African-American working-class cultural expression) versus the way they respond to country. The blues has been commodified and exoticized by the dominant white elite, and the blues "works" because white audience members can keep Black performers at a "safe" distance as Other—poor, downtrodden, and dark-skinned. Hearing about African Americans in poverty and in distress reassures the white audience that they are in no danger of joining the performers in their downtrodden condition. Partly because the distance white audience members perceive and/or construct between themselves and performers is so wide, they don't hear these songs of loss and identify with them.

This doesn't work so well with country music, because within a racist framework, whiteness pulls the audience members closer to the performers. Class-privileged white audience members actually *hear* these messages about continual loss and confront the possibility that they, too, will lose. The closeness is uncomfortable, especially these days, when even upper-middle-class people are beginning to feel the rampant insecurity most of us live with because of the capitalist system. They can't respond, as they do with the blues, by pushing it all away. It creeps too close to home.

3. *"Country music drives me crazy. It's so sentimental."*

"Sentimental" comes from "sentiment," which in turn comes from the Latin word *sentire*, "to perceive by the senses and the mind, to feel, to think."[9] In and of itself, then, sentimentality is not bad. But a negative meaning has become attached to it through decades of art standards imposed by Western art critics. Within their parameters, sentimentality receives a big thumbs down. Objectivity, distance, and detachment—between the artist and his/her work, between the viewer and the work, between the critic and the work—are characteristics to strive for. Excessive attachment, care, feeling and passion of any sort mark the work of an immature, undeveloped, and unsuccessful artist; they also mark the wrong characteristics to uphold when viewing art.

These particular art standards don't begrudge *all* emotion. There's a context for acceptable emotion. It's fine, even appropriate, to be moved to detached "rapture" by classical music, but if, for example, the Iris DeMent song quoted above evokes a sad memory of separation from home and family, sparks a sentimental response—that's not so fine. Up-close, personal, and inherently excessive (that scary word again) sentimentality is bad. Which is why country music emerges as a clear loser when measured against these standards. The history of country music is a history of songs written and performed by a person who pulls subject matter from personal experience or experiences of friends and family members. Reactions, thoughts, and feelings are woven into the song. Sentimentality runs rampant. Listeners are *meant* to feel what the performer feels.

The depth of feeling in country-western music astounds me, particularly when I hear what sounds like genuine grief and joy in early country music. And this is not surprising. Throughout my life I've consistently observed more authentic emotions from working-class and working-poor people than I have from middle-class and upper-class people. I'm not romanticizing or essentializing us in making this observation, or suggesting that working-class people have it all together emotionally. I think we express more of our feelings because we haven't had manners, refinement, and the "social graces" of carefully meting out feelings and responses drilled into us since childhood. In our own personal lives, and in our cultural expressions, we convey what we feel in our hearts. This authentic emotion is not masked by walls of respectability.[10]

My own criteria for examining art and culture take into account the artist's feelings about form and content. I respect artistic and cultural expressions where passion is integrated into the work, and this is one reason country music ranks so high with me. As I'm writing this, I'm listening to Dwight Yoakam sing "Send a Message to my Heart."

> *Darlin when you're all alone*
> *Tell me do you think of me*
> *Does my name touch your lips*
> *Am I still in your dreams*
> *Do your arms reach out for mine*
> *In the still of the night*
> *Do you wish that I was with you*
> *When you turn out the light*
>
> *Send a message to my heart*
> *on the wings of the wind*
> *Let me hear your sweet voice sayin*
> *you love me again*
> *Even though we're apart*
> *I hold to your memory*
> *Send a message to my heart*
> *to keep you here with me.*[11]

4. "Those rednecks are so conservative! How can you listen to that crap?"

A close variation on this theme is the "George Bush likes country music—that's all I need to know" comment, which doesn't make logical sense. The political worldview of one listener doesn't point to an intrinsic flaw in the music. But the comment about Bush makes sense because so many people—politically progressive middle-class people in particular—understand country music as right-wing (meaning oppressively conservative) in nature, and intensely racist and sexist.

These commentators don't have the full picture. It's true that oppressive attitudes appear in country music, that songs reinforcing and condoning sexism and racism are popular, and that several country-western singers support causes such as no choice on abortion and school prayer. Why the shock? Within any large group participating in a similar cultural tradition, a variety of political opinions and ideologies exists. No one expects classical musicians to share a common political viewpoint.

However, to notice only those problematic elements bypasses what I have consistently noticed: country music exhibits predominantly left-wing[12] tendencies, albeit left-wing tendencies as defined by working-class people. These tendencies differ from the middle-class white left wing with its pro-peace, pro-disarmament, anti-gun stance that is for the most part neutral toward capitalism, that favors feminism in which women gain footholds in "respectable," middle-class professions, that holds a romanticized view of Mother Earth, and that encourages sensitivity among (middle-class) men. This analysis, while progressive and useful is some ways, is a class-bound ideology lacking an understanding not only of class issues but of race.[13]

Left-wing tendencies among working-class people differ markedly. The anti-war and anti-military position is usually absent, because the military provides benefits and job security.[14] Added to the pro-military position is a strong anti-police and anti-government sentiment. A critique of the capitalist system runs through this ideology. Women working lousy jobs for the sake of survival are honored; they aren't encouraged to look for middle-class jobs, because that's not an option for either working-class women or working-class men.

The specific example of attitudes toward prostitution shows the difference between left-wing middle-class and working-class ideologies. Before the advent of feminism, prostitution horrified progressive middle-class people. They wanted it to end, and often behaved in a patronizing manner toward the women involved. Recently, a (middle-class) feminist analysis has emerged; in many cases, feminists are responding to working-class members of organizations who have provided information and opinions about this issue from the women who actually do the work. Now there are more feminists who, examining prostitution through the lens of male and capitalist domination, understand the class and race dynamics of young, working-class/working-poor white women and women of color taking on this job.

This more adequate analysis copies the left-wing working-class analysis of prostitution, which situates prostitution within the context of capitalism (one more *really* lousy job), celebrates the women who survive, thumbs its nose at moralistic middle-class attitudes that condemn without understanding, and relays the women's stories and perspectives. Many country songs illustrate this. In the song "Fancy," written by Bobbie Gentry, for example, a desperately poor, dying woman spends the last of her money on a dress for her young daughter. She hopes the girl can work as a prostitute, and survive:

> *Now in this world there's a lot of self-righteous hypocrites*
> *That would call me bad*
> *And criticize Mama for turning me out*
> *No matter how little we had*
>
> *But though I ain't had to worry bout nothing*
> *For nigh on fifteen years*
> *I can still hear the desperation in my poor*
> *Mama's voice ringing in my ear*
>
> *She said, here's your one chance Fancy don't let me down*
> *Here's your one chance Fancy don't let me down*
> *Lord, forgive me for what I do*

But if you want out well it's up to you
Now don't let me down
Your Mama's gonna help you uptown.

While I believe left-wing tendencies generally prevail within country music, the predominant view is that all country singers are oppressively right-wing. This idea is part and parcel of an even more insidious stereotype about all working-class/working-poor people. We are commonly perceived as staunch believers in oppressive ideologies in ways middle- and upper-class people are not. White working-class communities are perceived as more racist, more sexist, and more homophobic than white middle-class communities. Working-class communities of color are perceived to be more sexist and more homophobic than white and colored middle-class communities. Running in close concert with this is the idea that the liberal tolerance expressed in (some) white middle-class/upper-class communities is the pinnacle of anti-op-pression work, the most we marginalized folks can hope for.

These misperceptions disturb me for many reasons, and while I respond to them in more depth in "Homophobic Workers or Elitist Queers?," I want to make some brief points here. First, these misperceptions are misperceptions, that is, they're not true. Second, they shore up the position of the dominant white elite by directing the focus away from where it should be—the oppressive ideas and practices of those in power. Third, the alleged virtuous tolerance of the middle and upper classes is held up as an ideal and an appropriate remedy to oppression. This is patently ridicu-lous. Fourth, these misperceptions work to reinforce racist/classist beliefs about particular communities in a backhanded but effective way, by keeping working-class people divided and weak, and by keeping middle-class people from closely scrutinizing their com-munities for problematic ideologies and practices.
5. *"They're just like us after all! Whew!"*

Recently, I've heard many sighs of relief about country music's crossover into a more mainstream following. Within the past few years, the music has made a remarkable resurgence, attracting more and more northern middle-class followers. More country-western radio stations have sprung up in areas where middle-class and upper-middle-class people live. Many of the people I clean for—yuppies in particular—sport collections of Vince Gill and Garth Brooks. I've heard some people connect this to the nation's move to the right, while others believe that in this time of social upheaval, family breakdown, and rising divorce rates, the "traditional family values" of country music appeal to more and more people. (I find this attitude particularly amusing in light of the long country-western tradition of songs discussing, as a matter of course, unwed mothers, prostitution, absent fathers, infidelity, and lousy marriages.)

I'm unsure of why this is happening. Did this "newfound" popularity (that is, nothing exists until rich people know about it) come from successful marketing? Did executives in the music industry sense that intense marketing might reap high profits? Or was it that the music began resonating for more people, and the industry happily jumped on board? Is it a combination of these two factors? While I don't know why it's happening, I do know I'm wary of this popularity. If there's a chance for a more middle-class, "respectable" following, *and* higher profits, the artists whose work will be promoted and given air time will surely be de-politicized musicians without much twang. The southern, rural, and working-class roots of the music will be ignored or made fun of. There is some evidence that this is already happening. Artists like Iris DeMent—twangy, traditional, and working-class left-wing—are never played on commercial radio. Anti-southern jokes have been heard on new country stations. Artists with questionable musical talent, offering a form of pop-country, are given far too much air time.

The capitalist system has a terrifying ability to destroy artforms by severing them from their roots and sanitizing them of their radical streak. Some days I fear that could happen to country music. This would be especially painful and ironic, given country music's history of providing a sharp and precise critique of capitalism, from Loretta Lynn's "Coal Miner's Daughter" to Aaron Tippin's "Workin Man's Ph.D."

And me? I put on country music when I cook supper for my family. I turn my radio up loud and sing with Aaron Tippin and Winona Judd as I drive home after a day of cleaning. I revel in the excessive sentiment of the music and appreciate its telling portraits of the lives of people like me. I warm up to some people because they tell me how exciting it was to drive by Reba McEntire's horse farm while in Tennessee, and I pull away from others who look askance and say, "You like that crap?" I listen to Hank Williams:

Hear that lonesome whippoorwill
He sounds too blue to fly
The midnight train is whinin low
I'm so lonesome I could cry

I've never seen a night so long
when time goes crawlin by
The moon just went behind the clouds
to hide its face and cry

Did you ever see a robin weep
when leaves begin to die
that means he's lost the will to live
I'm so lonesome I could cry

The silence of a fallen star
lights up a purple sky
and as I wonder where you are
I'm so lonesome I could cry.

notes

1. Thanks to three gals who love country music for their help with this piece—Jan Binder, Elliott (who celebrates her birthday the same day Johnny Cash celebrates his!), and Eleanor Savage.
2. I believe a privileged white elite sets the standards for art in this country, and thus it stands to reason any working-class cultural form would be dismissed. These standards need to be challenged on the basis of racism, classism, sexism, and other oppressions, and critical questions asked about whether they hold any relevance whatsoever.
3. I am aware, however, that the same thing often happens to people who listen to rap music.

4. At first I feared that setting the essay up with this format would produce a reactive piece. But instead, this framework offers a door into country music that allows me to point out some of the positive aspects of working-class culture embodied in this art form.

5. These ballads were often women's ballads, reflecting songs of love, heartbreak, and unfaithfulness. This history has a lot to do with the fact that country music has, from the beginning, been open to women's stories. Thus, far from being the most sexist music, as its detractors love to claim, country has had more space for women's experiences than many other popular music forms. Thanks to Elliott for raising this point.

6. Thanks, Jan.

7. While I support white working-class/working-poor people who reclaim this term, I also want to point out the insidious and common ways it is used by rich people to put down poor people. I'm using it the latter way here.

8. Thanks to Jan Binder for raising this point.

9. *Webster's New International Dictionary*, Second Edition.

10. Thanks to Jan Binder and Nasreen Mohammed for helping me articulate this point.

11. It was a real trip runnin the spell-check on this essay. I typed quotations from songs as accurately as I could, and so wrote sayin instead of saying. I didn't write sayin' because the apostrophe indicates that something is missin—in this case, the "ing" ending used by middle-class/upper-class people in their speech as opposed to the "in" working-class ending. The spell-check, of course, read all of these words—lookin, sayin, dancin—as misspelled. Who programmed these computers?

12. I use the word "left-wing" here instead of "progressive" because progressive, while helpful in some ways, always feels to me like a middle-class, middle-of-the-road word that doesn't capture the strength and depth I include when discussing left-wing people and ideas. This is a personal preference.

13. In my brief discussion here of middle-class and working-class left-wing tendencies, I'm simply sketching an overview of commonly held viewpoints. This isn't an exhaustive analysis, nor do all group members share every idea I list.

14. This is a subject that deserves more analysis. The left-wing working-class tendencies differ markedly from country to country. For example, in Canada the working-class left-wingers are strongly anti-military. This is in large part because Canada has a tiny army. There've been very few jobs for working-class people in the army, and pro-army rhetoric has never been a big deal.

Catholic School Days

sketch number three

A good person would have wanted to hold Inez Fournier's hand during group games. No matter how hard I tried I didn't want to, but I forced myself. I wanted to be good. The part of me that wanted to be good fought with the part of me that wanted to give Inez and her sister, Therese, and Gerda O'Neill and her dozens of sisters and brothers, and the Macdonald girls as wide a berth as I could. I didn't want to touch poverty.

"Inez has fleas," boys and girls hissed, cruelly and calmly and assuredly. "Inez has fleas. If you touch her, you'll get them."

"Go to hell," was her stock reply. I respected this. At the same time, I couldn't understand the flea comment. Inez didn't have fleas. Animals had fleas. Animals caught them from hanging out in fields where fleas lived. If your dog visited such a field, she might start scratching. Entirely random, it was simply the luck of the draw whether your animal caught fleas.

If your dog ended up with a bad case, it was tough getting rid of them. People worked hard, bathing the dog, washing bedding, cleaning the whole house. Sometimes this did the trick and the pesky fleas vanished, but sometimes it didn't. Entirely random, it was simply the luck of the draw whether your family got rid of the critters.

Even though we hung out in the same field, Inez's family caught poverty and mine didn't. A random event. They tried really hard to get rid of it. Her father and mother both held full-time-plus jobs, and so did her sixteen-year-old brother, Marcel. But no matter how hard they worked, they couldn't make poverty disappear. My family worked hard, and we were not poor. The luck of the draw.

Fear lurked within our luck. Fear clung to my parents, who grew up the way Inez did. My parents, and other working-class parents I knew, dealt with fear by clinging to union jobs, depositing paychecks immediately, scrutinizing bank balances, planning carefully, spending money even more carefully. They focused eyes straight ahead, never behind. Sometimes they took furtive glances to the left and right but mostly they looked ahead, and that's what they taught us.

"It's been a hard day's night, and I been workin like a dog," Inez hummed during math class. I had trouble concentrating on long division problems. "It's been a hard day's night, I should be sleepin like a log."

To glance at Inez, during math class or any other time, meant looking behind, meant looking in the wrong direction. I peeked anyway and it scared me. Failing grades, scorn from teachers and students, icky clothes. I felt miserable in hand-me-downs that never hung right, but Inez had to alternate between two sagging shifts—shapeless house dresses—just like her mother always wore. Our mothers threw these on for housecleaning but wouldn't be caught dead with them in public. No, that would be shameful. Two shifts for Inez. One dull pink, one nasty green.

"Nice dress," someone taunted.

"Go to hell," Inez responded calmly as she pulled on skates two sizes too big; she skated rings around all of us. "Love, love me, do." Inez adored the Beatles and sang whenever the mood struck. Where did she get the nerve? "You know I love you." Even Liz Allen, whose parents paid for lessons, couldn't hold a candle to Inez. "I'll always be true." Inez yanked her straight, long hair free from the plain elastic. I fingered the band holding my pony-tail in place, the kind that didn't tear hair that you bought at the drugstore. "So please, love me, do."

Inez pursed her lips so tightly together it looked like they might close in on themselves. She squinted her eyes, which were actually large and hazel and pretty, but never got glasses. She was my age but looked three or four years older. I wondered if poverty speeded up time and rushed the years along, since her mother also appeared a good ten years older than anyone else's mother. I noticed other differences. Mrs. Fournier had no wedding band or engagement ring, even though she was married and had presumably been engaged. This marked her. Mrs. Fournier had crooked teeth, and this did not mark her. Even parents with union membership had come into the dental plan too late to do their teeth any good. Mrs. Fournier had given birth to three children, Marcel, Therese, and Inez. Marcel had already dropped out of school. Therese, a grade ahead of us, was even skinnier than Inez. She looked hungry all the time, even after lunch.

"It's such a long walk." I heard Inez explaining her daily routine to her one friend, Jane. The Fourniers lived further away than anyone else, except Gerda and her huge batch of siblings. Mr. and Mrs. Fournier rented a tiny house on a block of rundown bungalows. "At 7:30 we walk a mile along Taunton, then catch the Simcoe Street bus. Right now it's the worst. When we get off the bus to walk home it's totally dark."

I knew that stretch of Taunton Road. No sidewalks, no lights. And this by no accident. Plus, here drivers always ignored the speed limit and stepped heavily on the gas pedal.

When she was walking home one winter night, Therese was hit by a car. She happened to be nearest the road and Inez happened to be the lucky survivor. The driver dragged Therese hundreds of yards but never stopped. Inez could only remember a quiet motor, which meant the owner didn't live nearby. People shook their heads and said, "It's impossible to drag a body that far and not know you're doing it."

I pictured a man in a suit, one hand on the steering wheel, the other draped casually across the front seat. I pictured a well-fed man with straight teeth and a spanking-new wallet with lots of twenty-dollar bills.

Inez ran half a mile for help, on the dark, cold road. She fell and ripped her tights and cut her knees. I noticed this the next day, because even though her sister had been assaulted in a hit-and-run accident, her parents still didn't have money for new tights. Therese lay in a coma for a month, then died.

That same day Inez told Sister Ann Richard, "I need to sit out. My knees hurt." I skated by the bench several times but Inez wasn't singing "I Wanna Hold Your Hand." She looked sad but not surprised. The only girls who ever looked surprised had fathers who worked in the office at general motors. But the rest of us knew enough not to be shocked. We had it worse because our fathers worked the line and because we weren't boys. No one said poor boys had fleas.

For even with her tragedy and unmoved face, boys and girls still whispered, "Inez has fleas," and she still said, "Go to hell." Things remained this way until high school, when we parted ways. Even then I heard about Inez, because in our small city news traveled. At least some news did. Inez finished Grade 10. She didn't leave because of pregnancy; it seemed poverty in and of itself cut her education short.

I thought about Inez and her family, now minus one skinny sister, and I thought about the two of us. Our lives had forked away from each other and yet stayed close. Close enough that the smell of poverty scared me. Close enough to know I didn't want to embrace Inez. Close enough to know the space between us did not exist and it did exist.

Kids taunted Inez because they feared what happened to her could happen to them. We didn't stand together and resist capitalism's divide-and-conquer strategy. No. Divided then, divided now. And not by any force of nature. Neither did a force of nature release the fleas, or fence the field, or decide one small field provided more than enough space for all of us.

Fleas, hands, poverty. Lessons in a school yard. The moral ramifications of hand holding. The causal connection between fleas and poverty. The luck of the draw. The gamble that back-breaking hard work twelve hours a day might do something for your family or it might do nothing at all.

"Inez has fleas," someone whispered. Yes, I thought, and we're all hanging out in the same field.

Moving From Cultural Appropriation Toward Ethical Cultural Connections[1]

My grandmother trudged from the hills of rural Lebanon to the shores of the Mediterranean, carrying clothes and a derbeke.[2] She and the drum survived several weeks in the steerage compartment of a large boat. No small feat. And now she's dead, and the derbeke sits on a shelf far away from me. But I ended up with my sittee's determination, which I've needed to navigate through the stormy waters of drumming.

After experiencing so much anti-Arab hatred growing up, I cut myself off from my culture as soon as I could. I tried hard to assimilate, with the attendant craziness and confusion; but thankfully, my journey into political awareness and action brought me back to my racial/cultural heritage, and in particular to its music. Hearing familiar rhythms, I found myself thinking about—and wanting—a brass derbeke with a chrome finish and intricate engraving. Just like the one my grandmother brought from Lebanon.

So my lover and I embarked on a grand search to ferret out my derbeke. It took a long time, partly because I didn't know where to look, partly because white people's interest in drumming hadn't fully impacted the market. In January 1991, a year after the search began, Jan and I marched in Washington, D.C. to protest the slaughter of Arabs in the vicious outbreak of U.S. imperialism known as the Gulf War. During that weekend, alternating between grief and numbness, we chanced upon a store specializing in musical instruments from around the world. I found my derbeke.

The end of my search? No. Just the beginning. Now I needed a teacher and a community that would offer technical assistance and political respect. I attended drumming workshops, but each proved as problem-laden as my first, where I found an overwhelmingly white group of women who apparently hadn't given much thought to the issue of playing congas or derbekes. I'm using the word "play" loosely, because even as an unskilled beginner I could tell these women didn't know the traditional Arabic techniques and rhythms I knew simply from listening to Arabic music. Further dismay resulted when I questioned two women and discovered they didn't know the name of their drums; they had just been drawn to the derbeke for some unknown reason and made a purchase. They spent the workshop banging happily on their drums in ways bearing no resemblance to proper derbeke-playing style.

I sat through this drumming workshop, and subsequent ones, with a familiar mix of anger and fear. Anger at the casual (mis)use by white people of important aspects of culture from various communities of color, fear that such groups would prove the only resource available and I would simply have to put up with crap in order to learn. These disheartening experiences led to another year of my derbeke gathering dust as I grew more certain I'd never find what I needed.

But after much searching, I found a wonderful teacher, Mick Labriola, as well as drumming friends/acquaintances I connect with politically and musically. Because of this, and because of my deep determination to forge ahead in spite of obstacles, drumming has proved an incredibly positive experience. I've re-connected with my roots. Experiencing how much beauty and importance Arabs have given the world has helped me feel pride, as opposed to shame, about being Arab.

Then there's anger and grief. My initial experiences at drumming workshops proved common. I continually see derbekes in white people's homes, played by white musicians, banged on at drumming circles. Many players don't even know the name of the instrument, or where it comes from. They don't play properly, and they don't know traditional Arabic rhythms.

But none of this seems to raise any concern, as more and more white people jump on the drumming bandwagon. Why drumming? Why so popular? Because it's a powerful activity? Because it's a wonderfully communal instrument? Because it allows people to learn about other cultures through music? Most days I think these explanations provide a more positive interpretation than the situation warrants, especially when I notice the apolitical spirituality of the New Age movement embracing the concept of "getting in touch with inner rhythms" via the drums of people of color; white people dredding their hair and buying African drums; people "playing" an instrument without knowing its name.

Within these actions, I sense an imperialist attitude in which privileged people want to own segments of other people's cultures. To me, it's cultural appropriation, a subject I'm confused about and infuriated by. I have many questions and ideas, but few answers. The complexity of the subject lends itself more to books (*not* written by white people) than single essays, so be forewarned; I can't tackle everything. I've tried to streamline this by focusing it around drumming, and in particular derbekes, since issues and questions relating to drumming carry over to other types of cultural appropriation.

❖　◆　❖　◆　❖　◆　❖

I've thought long and hard about defining cultural appropriation. Culture includes any and all aspects of a community that provide its life force, including art, music, spirituality, food, philosophy, and history. To "appropriate" means to take possession of. "Cultural" appropriation means taking possession of specific aspects of someone else's culture in unethical, oppressive ways.

117

While helpful, this basic definition simplifies rather than deepens. It doesn't examine various aspects of cultural appropriation. To do that, I'll analyze what happens when white people play derbekes incorrectly.

It seems to me those white people use derbekes perceiving them as generic, no-name drums unencumbered by hard political/historical/cultural realities, never asking themselves the questions that would uncover these realities, such as: whose music is this? What has imperialism and racism done to the people who created this music? Do I have a right to play this instrument? What kind of beliefs do I hold about Arabs? Ignoring these questions and ignoring Arab musical traditions translates into cultural appropriation—white people taking possession of Arabic culture by commandeering an important instrument and the music it produces. The derbeke and its playing style are important pieces of Arab culture, with thousands of years of history attached. To disregard that and play however one chooses whitewashes the drum, and by implication Arab culture. When stripped of its historical legacy, the drum is placed outside Arab culture, suggesting that Arab culture and history aren't worth taking seriously; even though Arabs have created something valuable and life-enhancing in our music, that doesn't matter. White people can and will choose to perceive the drum as ahistorical and culturally empty—a plaything that can be given whatever meaning the player chooses.

To perceive a derbeke as a plaything is to carry the privileged attitude that has wrought devastation all over our planet: "Everything is here for me to play with and use." Whether peoples, lands, or cultures, it's there for the grabbing. This take-take-take attitude pushed white colonizers through whole peoples and lands on the Asian, African, and American continents. Although brown, black, and yellow people filled those continents, white people perceived them as empty.

That kind of colonization continues, and new forms have evolved. The colonialist attitude has affixed itself to our music, clothing, religions, languages, philosophies and art. I overheard a white shopper in a music store examining a derbeke. "Cool drum. I'll take a couple." He perceived the derbeke as an empty vessel waiting to have meaning infused into it, as opposed to an important cultural symbol/reality embodying centuries of meaning.

I don't believe every white person who buys a derbeke holds that attitude, or that no other issues or desires are mixed in. But I do believe large and small vestiges of colonialist ideas live in many places, and it frightens and angers me. These ideas and their practice have already destroyed so many of our people and may well destroy more. Many white people don't know they possess such a mindset, and unthinking, unexamined ignorance can cause irreparable harm.

These political questions must be raised, along with the psychological effects of cultural appropriation. Many times people of color gloss over these, possibly because we don't want to admit the extent of our pain. I want to try.

Cultural appropriation causes me anger and grief. Anger about flagrant disregard and disrespect for me and my community, about unexamined privilege and power, about cavalier white people who use important cultural symbols/realities and turn them into no-name items. And grief, which stems from a hopeless, powerless feeling that I/my community will never get the respect and consideration we deserve, that no matter how hard we struggle, no one hears our words or heeds our demands.

Along with those responses is one that so far hasn't been examined in our thinking and writing about cultural appropriation; for me this causes deep pain. Cultural appropriation cuts away at and undermines my basic racial identity.

It's been hard for me to create a clear, strong identity as Arab-American. It's been hard for me to believe I really exist as such a person, when dominant society categorically trivializes, diminishes, and whitewashes Arabs. I've struggled with this for years, and recently my identity has been strengthened, thanks in part to my derbekes. They help me realize I come from somewhere, my community exists, and we've created wonderful cultural expressions over the centuries.

When, as happens frequently, I come across the attitude that clearly says the derbeke is an empty vessel, I begin doubting myself and my community, doubting our very existence. I fight constantly against internalizing the message—if the derbeke means nothing, if it comes from nowhere, I don't exist.

❖   ●   ❖   ●   ❖   ●   ❖

It's impossible to examine increased derbeke sales or the increased numbers of white "shamans" without discussing multiculturalism. Strange things are happening under the guise of "honoring diversity," because multiculturalism, as defined and practiced by white people, is partly responsible for the increase in cultural appropriation. While I'm not opposed to *authentic* multiculturalism, I do believe unauthentic or artificial or perverse multiculturalism simply feeds and reinforces imperialist attitudes. Examples of this abound. Young white schoolchildren aren't taught to connect ethically with other cultures; they're taught to take whatever they want from other cultures and *use* it. White adult consumers snatch our various arts, wanting the stuff but not caring if its creators are systematically destroyed.

Given the brutal racism endemic to our society, it makes sense that much of what passes for multiculturalism is actually covert and overt cultural appropriation, actually a form of cultural genocide. As dominant white society casually buys and sells our symbols/realities, their cultural meaning is watered down and their integrity diminished. Today items from various communities of color are all the rage, but I'm not happy to see the walls of white people's homes adorned with African masks, Asian paintings, and Native ceremonial objects. Behind the rhetoric and hype about multiculturalism and honoring diversity lurk the same attitudes of entitlement and privilege that form part of structural racism. For the most part, these white people haven't done the work necessary to become allies to people of color. They know little or nothing about current global struggles of people of color, as we define and articulate them. They don't engage in acts of solidarity around specific issues such as Native self-determination or Palestinian liberation. They don't read books by radical authors of color.

Further, these white people haven't analyzed a monster related to racism, that is, classism and the global capitalist system. All of us need to be clear about how and where and why the capitalist system fits into the picture. We need to ask critical questions. Is "multiculturalism" the latest capitalist fad? Who's in control? Who's benefiting? And who's making money, now that it's popular to hang Native dream webs on bedroom walls? Could it be people of color? Hardly. As more and more people of color are forced to live on the streets, white entrepreneurs are getting rich selling our art, music, and spirituality. Watching them profit as they exploit and appropriate our cultures, when for years we experienced hostility and scorn trying to preserve them in a racist society, is truly galling. I grew up with white people belittling and "joking" about my family's choice of music and dancing; now I can watch those same people rush to sign up for "real" belly-dancing lessons. Taught by a white woman, of course.

Economics impact culture, as the belly dance example shows. The particular combination of racism and classism that has popularized belly dancing taught by white people has several implications for Arab-American culture. Arab dancers who can't make a living teaching may be eventually forced to give up their serious studies of traditional dance altogether; this is one factor that eventually leads to cultural genocide. If a certain type of belly dancing becomes popular and another particular strain never catches on with white teachers, the latter could slowly disappear. Again, this factors into cultural genocide. For every cultural form happily adopted by the dominant culture's racist and classist system, another falls by the wayside. Some expressions discarded by dominant society will continue to thrive among marginalized communities, some will be lost forever.

Further, class exploitation crosses over with racism in certain ways, and thus many people of color are working-class or work-ing-poor. Consequently, we can't afford to buy the now-available music, paintings, instruments, and books from our cultures. We can't afford travel to our countries of origin. Observing white, middle-class people engaging in these activities adds yet another layer of anguish and complexity to these issues.

Recently I talked over the phone with a white, middle-class man who has traveled extensively in various Arab countries, attended Arabic language schools, and now speaks Arabic fluently. Upon discovering I was Arab-American, he began speaking Arabic to me.

As is all too usual, I got so choked up with rage I couldn't think clearly. I said curtly, "I don't speak Arabic," and hung up. Next time, I have a response all planned out: "Gee, if only my grandparents hadn't experienced so much racism and been so isolated! Then they wouldn't have tried to assimilate. Then they would have taught us to speak Arabic. Which would be so helpful these days, now that multiculturalism is in. For those who can afford it, which of course precludes most people of color. Oh well, I hope you're having a splendid time with it all."

❖   •   ❖   •   ❖   •   ❖

The discussion of cultural appropriation between white people and people of color is critically important, but I want to push further. If we keep the focus on relationships between colored and white, we come up with an overly simplistic analysis that ignores the fact that many people of color are just as inattentive to these issues and thus act inappropriately toward each other. It implies the only groups worth discussing are *the* white people and *the* people of color, two broad categories which are sometimes helpful but also present problems in terms of understanding the complexities of race. These simplistic categories feed into the myth that people of color constitute a monolithic group unscathed by differences of skin color, immigrant status, gender, ability, sexuality, language, class, and religion. Further, reductionist categories support the lie that we can only be discussed in relation to white people, that our only important relationships exist with white people.

A simplistic analysis of cultural appropriation minimalizes and trivializes what we as people of color from different communities do to each other, glossing over the fact that we can and do commit acts of cultural appropriation, and thus hurt each other badly. I've had the painful experience of watching other people of color using derbekes as no-name drums. Our racial identity doesn't rule out unjust acts toward each other. If I were drawn to an African mask in a store and bought it without knowing where it came from, what it represents, and who made it, would that be acceptable? Of course not. I'd be committing an act of cultural appropriation as surely as any white person who did the same thing.

Our existence as people of color doesn't mean we know much—if anything—about other communities of color. It doesn't mean we've done the hard work of freeing ourselves from stereotypes and lies about other racial/ethnic groups. I've heard, time and again, the same kind of anti-Arab racism out of the mouths of people of color that I've heard from white people. Unless people of color do the same anti-racist work we want white people to do, we can't become true allies and friends.

However, I don't equate the actions of people of color with those of white people. There's a difference between a white person and a person of color playing derbekes incorrectly. The white person's actions feed into structural racism; they're part and parcel of the systemic oppression by white people of people of color. The person of color's actions stem, I think, from a mix of structural racism and horizontal violence in which the dominant white power structure keeps us carefully divided from each other, duplicating their mistreatment, and ignorant about the many ways our lives connect.

Even with this understanding, it still hurts when a Latino uses a derbeke as a generic drum. In some ways, because I so badly want and need solidarity from other people of color, these actions hurt more. I don't expect as much from white people, so I'm not as shocked and hurt by their actions. But betrayal from other people of color cuts deeply.

Betrayal appears in varied forms, and I briefly want to mention sexism. Many men of color bring a problematic and divisive note to discussions of drumming and culture by insisting women can't drum because it's not "traditional." I have two responses to this. First, there's historical documentation from many cultures, including Arabic ones, of women drumming in earlier times. Second, even in relation to preserving our cultures,

I find the label "traditional" almost irrelevant. If women didn't drum in the past, why would we want to carry on with that aspect of our culture? Are the men who propose this anxious to continue every traditional cultural practice, from the most inane to the most misogynist?[3] Plenty of manifestations of sexism and misogyny in Arab cultures need to be kissed goodbye.

❖ • ❖ • ❖ • ❖

As a person of color, I want to do more than react to oppression by white people. It's important that, as a subject and moral agent with power in the world, I state what I want and what I consider acceptable. For starters, do I want to share cultural traditions?

There are several reasons I do. First, when healthy cultural connections occur, it's personally and communally affirming. Someone has taken the time and energy to understand and appreciate the derbeke. She's taken me and my community/culture seriously, and shown respect. This affirms me and helps strengthen racial identity.

Second, I'm enriched by participating in an authentic multiculturalism that involves having friends, listening to the music, learning the histories, and being allies in struggle with people from various cultures. This type of multiculturalism has, at its root, respect, thoughtfulness, a political analysis, and openness.

Third, in practical terms, I don't know how to separate. I was born of an interracial marriage. I live in a racially mixed community and belong to organizations and groups that cut across cultures. I've read and listened to and integrated perspectives of people from different racial/ethnic communities. How to undo this mixing? Forget the books, the stories, the poems, the music that have become part of me? Give up friends? Return to my places of origin—which isn't physically possible, and where I may not feel at home for other reasons? It seems foolhardy to consider this.

I support the idea of sharing across cultures, but I also believe some things should never be shared. For starters, sacred instruments, rhythms, and rituals. Yet, unbelievably, this has happened, continues to happen. Several years ago I attended a music festival where two white women planned to perform with a sacred instrument from a community of Australian indigenous people. Although an Australian aboriginal woman was present and voiced objections, it didn't matter to the musicians. At the last minute, outcries from a larger group prevented the show. I don't know if these two musicians used the instrument other times, but given the depth of their resistance to restriction of their "artistic freedom," I wouldn't be surprised if they did.

Of course, I question whether those women should have been performing at all, since their show consisted of playing instruments from various communities of color. I'm tired of seeing white people get the praise, money, and publicity from public performance. However, I can't deal with these questions and issues here. The topic needs an essay of its own and quite possibly its own book.

Back to making and preserving connections across communities. How to make such links? And what to call them? Words carry critical weight in liberation struggles. Naming ourselves and our desires is vital. The term "ethical cultural connection" embodies my ideas. It focuses clearly on culture, on the lifeforce of a community. "Connection" speaks to a freely-chosen bonding experience between two people or two groups. The adjective "ethical" clarifies the type of connection—one based on respect, justice, and integrity.

Ethical cultural connections are comprised of respect for the community involved, a desire to learn and take action, an openness to being challenged and criticized, a willingness to think critically about personal behavior, and a commitment to actively fighting racism. These cornerstones remain the same whether I'm getting to know one Native person or buying a carving from a Native museum. They apply to people of color and white people.

I've come to the conclusion that I'm not opposed to non-Arabs playing derbekes if it's done with respect, knowledge, and seriousness, and if these attitudes manifest themselves in concrete action. I want drummers to learn the derbeke's culture and history, and the proper way to play. And to take this knowledge a step further by actively countering the imperialism, racism, and genocide Arabs experience today. It's not enough to celebrate cultural difference by learning language, music, or history, when people's whole worlds are at risk.

Of course, this raises a critical question. How do I know if someone's doing those things? By watching? Maybe the person plays the derbeke correctly, maybe he knows Arab rhythms. But that doesn't tell me how much he knows and cares about my people.

I can only know for sure if I talk to the drummer. That's the only way any of us will know. Typing out guidelines or policing cultural events won't do it. We need to talk—across cultures and classes. I've spent days and days and days writing this essay, and months pondering it, and I've been unable to think of any other way to know where a person stands. My analysis doesn't help in isolation. It helps as we communicate across all racial groups— Asian (including Arabs), Latino, Native, African, and white.

And talking to one person won't cut it. I'm sure any white person interested in assuaging her conscience could find enough white-identified Arabs to assure her whatever she does with the derbeke is okay. There are many such people in all communities— people who for whatever reasons have become so alienated from their roots and their communities that they casually approve of the worst kinds of cultural appropriation. At the music festival I mentioned earlier, participants discussed cultural appropriation several times, and it appeared the women of color shared a clear and unified response. That is, until a well-known woman of color, a superb drummer, announced from the stage that anyone who wanted a drum from whatever culture should buy it and play it. So much for solidarity.

I don't want white people seeking out white-identified people of color to give them the stamp of approval. I want white people to talk to many people, including political activists. I want discussion around power and privilege, about who benefits from cultural appropriation and in what ways, about who will decide how cultural connections happen and what makes them ethical. I want discussion about actions and the meanings they carry.

In these discussions, participants need to take emotional reactions into account without letting them dictate the whole discussion. If I'm so sick and tired of watching non-Arabs thought-lessly pound away on derbekes, I might not notice when someone's doing it right. I might not even care. I'm entitled to my anger, but one person's emotions can't set the tone and agenda for these discussions.

❖   ◆   ❖   ◆   ❖   ◆   ❖

I believe politicized people of color and our white allies must start framing discussions with helpful guidelines that make sense to us. Discussions must be cross-cultural and focussed on tough questions about racism, classism, unauthentic multiculturalism, power, and privilege. And I suggest we include the ways in which personal experience can help frame critical thinking on cultural appropriation.

Looking at the five derbekes that now grace this home, I'm struck by the connection between my drumming and my political thinking. The deeper I go with one, the deeper I go with the other. The political analysis I push myself to do translates into more meaningful drumming. Playing the derbeke helps deal with the pain I experience around vivid examples of cultural appropriation. I offer this personal example not as a "feel-good," quick, on-the-surface remedy for oppression and cultural genocide, but rather as a somber statement of possibility. We can plumb the depths of the worst in our society while participating in meaningful cultural activities that ground us and keep hope alive.

notes

1. Many thanks to Jan Binder for her help with this article.
2. A *derbeke* (pronounced der-beck-ee) is a traditional Arabic hand drum. I've seen several different spellings, but this is the one I prefer. The drum is also known as a *dumbek* (pronounced doom-beck)—there are varied spellings for that word as well.
3. Another problem with this attitude is that it feeds into the dangerous lie/myth that cultures are static and unchanging entities.

Frightening Bedfellows

pop culture and imperialism

ife is strange. I'm watching Disney's *Aladdin* and studiously taking notes although my inclination is to remove the video and pitch it. I've already shuddered my way through one viewing, and to say I'm dreading this repeat is a gross understatement; I'm actually feeling nostalgia for the days when Arabs enjoyed total invisibility. To add insult to injury, the video won't play properly. I return to the store for an exchange. "Gettin too much use," the clerk informs me. How cheery to consider the Native, white, and African-American kids who frequent this store imbibing *Aladdin* over and over.

I start again and don't encounter technical difficulties, only emotional and political ones. This blatant bit of anti-Arab propaganda spins through ninety minutes of Western time. As it groans to a halt, I throw my notebook on the table, where it falls beside Edward Said's *Culture and Imperialism*, a 350-page, thoroughly researched treatise I finished reading just yesterday. I refuse to let my mind dwell on the numbers game: how does the ratio of *Aladdin* viewers compare to Said readers?

But I can't help checking my scrawls about *Aladdin* against those on *Culture and Imperialism*. Said clearly documents the horror of imperialism and the ways writers support it. Disney helps prepare young American minds to accept whatever forms of intervention U.S. big business/government might undertake in the Arab world. Disney thus provides—probably without meaning to—a perfect example that extends Said's explanation of the links between "classical" culture and imperialism into the realm of popular culture.

❖　•　❖　•　❖　•　❖

Edward Said is a brilliant thinker who's written several powerful and influential texts, including *Orientalism* and *The Question of Palestine*. In *Culture and Imperialism*, he makes an enormous contribution to our understanding of imperialism, which he defines this way: "At some very basic level, imperialism means thinking about, settling on, controlling land that you do not possess, that is distant, that is lived on and owned by others. For all kinds of reasons it attracts some people and often involves untold misery for others."[1] Said examines the type of imperialism carried out by British, French, and American forces during the nineteenth and early twentieth centuries. He believes these imperialist ventures differed from previous ones; they came hand in hand with an ideology that claims that imperialism benefits the unwashed, inferior hordes in backward countries and that civilized white benefactors actually provide a great service.

Said describes the ways those in power spread this particular piece of important misinformation. Western educators and christian missionaries forced the lies on the hordes in question, while back home in the "civilized" world, well-known fiction writers of the time did their bit. Their talents didn't necessarily extend to any ability to analyze, critique, and counter the powerful social institution of imperialism. Said examines the work of several authors, including Albert Camus and Jane Austen, to show how they espoused, supported, and reinforced imperialist beliefs about people of color.

In *Mansfield Park*, Jane Austen portrays life in the early 1800s for the wealthy Bertram family, who are materially maintained thanks to workers on their Antigua sugar plantation. Said believes Austen's tone and style give readers the impression that these plantations, sustained with slave labor, are simply a dreary necessity of life for rich English families. Sir Thomas Bertram is never shown at the Antigua plantation, and to Said this implies it's an inconvenient but necessary place to do business, much as having to drive to London would be. Said writes: "Having read *Mansfield Park* as part of the structure of an expanding imperialist venture, one cannot simply restore it to the canon of 'great literary masterpieces'—to which it most certainly belongs—and leave it at that. Rather, I think, the novel steadily, if unobtrusively, opens up a broad expanse of domestic imperialist culture without which Britain's subsequent acquisition of territory would not have been possible."[2]

Said also examines the work of Albert Camus, a Frenchman born and raised in Algeria who wrote about that country under French occupation. Said believes Camus' influential words aided France in its attempts to represent, inhabit, and possess the country.[3] In his well-known novel, *L'Etranger (The Stranger),* Camus depicts a society in which France controls all important institutions, no one raises an eyebrow over the deaths of nameless Arabs, and France's right to occupy and own this land stands unquestioned. Camus accurately describes this reality but doesn't critique it, and in so doing he supports France's century-old project of wiping out Algeria's populations.[4]

Said doesn't want *Mansfield Park* or *L'Etranger* removed from literary studies. He believes readers would benefit from learning to critically analyze messages the texts carry about whites' obligations to civilize inferior races on the African, Asian, and American continents.

❖　◆　❖　◆　❖　◆　❖

Said's call for critical analysis is worth heeding when viewing *Aladdin*. Basic story: a poor Arab boy finds a magic lamp and the genie inside grants three wishes. Basic analysis: a perverted and frightening view of Arab society. Here's one example from the movie's opening song:

> *I come from a land*
> *From a faraway place*
> *Where the caravan camels roam.*

> *Where it's black and immense and the heat is intense,*
> *It's barbaric but hey it's home.*

Bad enough, but a step above the original version. Arab Americans lobbied long and hard with Disney executives in a futile effort to get rid of the worst of *Aladdin*'s racism. One change resulted. The lines above initially read:

> *I come from a land*
> *From a faraway place*
> *Where the caravan camels roam.*
> *Where they cut off your ear*
> *If they don't like your face.*
> *It's barbaric, but hey, it's home.*

Aladdin presents dozens and dozens of "bad" Arabs, all grotesque, ugly, and sinister, with huge noses and strong accents. The "good" characters, Aladdin and Princess Jasmine, are for all intents and purposes white, in spite of dark skin—which isn't as dark as the others. With Caucasian features and white, middle-class American accents, they're as Arab as baseball and apple pie.

At first glance, differences between *Aladdin* and Said's text loom large. In contrast to Said's thoughtful research and clear thinking, Disney offers representation so stereotypical as to be absurd. Said's basic premise poses people of color as articulate, thinking, active subjects, while Disney assumes stupid, grotesque, passive objects. Said portrays the Arab world as thinking, changing, varied, resisting, while Disney renders it static, barbaric, uniform, and passive. And a quick read of *Aladdin* doesn't reveal its connection to imperialism, the subject of Said's work. No armies move in, no American soldiers gather on street corners, nothing suggests armed intervention or attacks against the Arab population. Yet *Aladdin* carries an important subtext about imperialism.

Knowing the context helps see this subtext. American government/big business has had imperialist designs on the Arab world since the 1930s. They want to control and exploit natural resources, particularly oil, and subdue Arab nationalism and organizing. They want to establish a military base in Saudi Arabia, and an important United States "victory" in the Gulf War was gaining a foothold there. Finally, the United States supports Israel and its expansionist aims; without American funding, Israel's occupations in Palestine and Lebanon would end in a day.

Add Said's thesis here: imperialism works better when citizens believe it will actually help the local population. This means American government/big business can't accomplish their goals in the Arab world unless they convince the American population that Arabs are patently unfit to govern land and control resources.

Films like *Aladdin* help relay that message, depicting Arabs as too stupid to control our own destiny, as incapable of making intelligent and healthy decisions about how to live on Arab land. *Aladdin* depicts backward "bad" Arabs filled with sinister violence who need Western guidance to move out of a barbaric society in which market vendors cut off the hands of women who steal for hungry children. (In case anyone's wondering, that doesn't happen in the Arab world). *Aladdin* reinforces the idea that the United States should and can move into the Arab world—as it moved into Iraq—and take over, because obviously Arabs can't run Arab countries. Even "good" Arab rulers, like Jasmine's father, need help, and who better fits the bill than smart Americans? The Sultan's childishness and naivete make him an easy mark for nasty men like Jafar. Better that white men in business suits control him than evil Arabs in turbans.

Through *Aladdin*, Disney is cultivating millions of young American minds to believe these lies about Arabs, and the cinematography strengthens its ability to get this message across to young children. The animation, cartoon quality, colors, and magical effects draw viewers in as *Aladdin* pitches its appeal on both conscious and subconscious levels.

Aladdin reeks of imperialism and racism. But that analysis doesn't take us far enough, since Disney also managed to pack in classism, sexism, and heterosexism. All these elements must be unpacked.

In *Aladdin*'s opening scene, a merchant offers a combination coffeemaker and hookah. Just what those drug-using, coffee-drinking Arabs want. This character exemplifies the way racism and classism work hand in hand. His greasy and sleazy nature spells Arab. His skills as a rip-off artist selling badly-made, questionable goods spell lazy poor person who really has it easy.

This character is connected to a group of men with unspecified occupations, who seem to represent a police force. They chase Aladdin after he steals a loaf of bread, and later pursue Jasmine and Aladdin. For any of these men, substitute other Disney cartoon representatives of stereotypically stupid workers—big, burly, dark, with missing teeth; their lack of smarts ranks so high that one middle-class boy and his monkey outwit them again and again. These men run into each other, bang heads, fall from roofs, but still press on with the job! Perfect workers. Even a damaged head (brain) won't prevent them from reporting to work next day.

And what about Aladdin himself? Theoretically a poor streetperson, in reality he acts, looks, and talks like a middle-class white American. Nothing speaks to hard times or a painful past, certainly not the self-confidence and entitlement he exudes. However, his alleged desperate class straits can be used when it suits his purpose, much like reaching for a favorite sweatshirt. During one allegedly frightening moment, the Genie says, "I can't help," but Aladdin jumps to the rescue: "I'm a street rat, remember? I'll improvise." The street smarts of working-class/working-poor people turn into a casual commodity this hero accesses whenever he chooses.

Aladdin's humble beginnings do complicate his life as the movie draws to a close. Even though he has saved the kingdom and triumphed over the evil Jafar, Aladdin can't receive his just reward—Jasmine, the object in question. After all, only princes have the right to marry princesses. Sniff, sniff. But the hankies can be put away and we can sigh with pleasure after all. Not because Jasmine or Aladdin rebel over elitist laws, but because the Sultan makes gracious, benevolent use of his power. He changes the law and allows the two lovebirds a chance to live happily ever after.

Funny how that old American dream—the poor man marrying the rich woman—shows up in a Disney version of an Arab folktale. Of course, the poor man only gets the princess because the powers that be take a personal liking to Aladdin and bend the rules his way. Probably without meaning to, the film accurately depicts how rags-to-riches stories really work—with plenty of help from above.

Untroubled by these problematic political messages, Aladdin and Jasmine race off into the sunset, a perfect image of happy heterosexuals. Or so we're led to believe. But can a heterosexual relationship built on male manipulation really lead to bliss? Throughout the movie, Aladdin disrespects Jasmine by lying to her, and continues even after Jasmine challenges him. What makes this doubly insidious is Disney's presentation of Jasmine as an independent woman searching for adventure. She indulges these whims for a brief while, then abandons them to cling to the arm of a man who treats her unethically.

Still, Jasmine, the lone upper-class female on the horizon, is more fortunate than her sisters. At least she talks now and again. To the best of my remembrance, only one other woman speaks. (I considered watching the movie a third time to verify this, but even as a conscientious movie reviewer, I couldn't.) The silent working-class women who grace the screen are fat, old, or middle-aged, "ugly," and toothless. We also glimpse young, slim, "pretty," toothy, and equally silent middle-class/upper-class women. This blatant sexism speaks far more loudly than Disney's P.R. claim of featuring strong female characters.

❖ ◆ ❖ ◆ ❖ ◆ ❖

Disney seems captivated by the Aladdin story, or perhaps by its profit margins. *The Return of Jafar*, a sequel to *Aladdin*, is now available in video stores, and the Genie character is back in a movie of his own. *Aladdin* paraphernalia leers from department store shelves, and I heard a vicious rumor about a Saturday morning *Aladdin* cartoon. Yuck.

Disney might want us to believe it's supporting multicultural-ism by re-telling *Aladdin*, since this story is touted as one of the Arabic folktales that make up *The Arabian Nights*. Story-telling is an important Arabic artform, and tellers have recounted lore from *The Arabian Nights* for hundreds and hundreds of years. In the last few centuries, these stories have been transferred to paper and made available in Arabic, French, English, and other languages.

Husain Haddawy grew up hearing his grandmother recite tales from *The Arabian Nights*. Years later, as a scholar, he took on the task of translating a collection of *The Arabian Nights* from Arabic into English. In Haddawy's introduction to this edition,[5] he notes that *Aladdin* doesn't appear in any known Arabic manu-script or edition of *The Arabian Nights*, nor among the eleven basic stories of *The Arabian Nights*. Neither had Haddawy heard the tale at his grandmother's knee, although he remembers all other eleven stories. After in-depth studies, Haddawy concluded that French scholars added *Aladdin* into the collection several centuries after the original manuscripts had been circulating. Haddawy says bluntly that *Aladdin*, as an Arabic folktale, is a forgery. The fact that *Aladdin* is likely a forged story slipped into a well-known collection of Arabic folktales adds yet another problematic dimension to Disney's problem-filled hit.

❖　◆　❖　◆　❖　◆　❖

Disney movies call out to me. They simply demand to be pitched far, far away. Their sexism, classism, racism, imperialism, and heterosexism appall me. The links between Walt Disney, the CIA, and fascism only strengthen these feelings. Not to mention kids of color in my neighborhood running around advertising Disney movies on their chests.

Seriously, these movies do call out to me. Why not establish a strong coalition of activists concerned about Disney messages? If we attempt to include people whose groups are portrayed problematically in these movies, we've got, for starters, Arab

Americans, Native Americans, feminists, working-class/working-poor people, queers, and general progressive types. Such groups could work on analyzing *all* messages in these movies, could offer an integrated analysis of the various stereotypes and dismal representations. They could also plan and carry out specific actions: target opening nights in major cities; devise presentations for community organizations such as parents' networks and teachers' groups; stage humorous street theater that sums up implicit and explicit messages in Disney movies; shoot their own videos where truly independent girls and sweet boys connect with their racial/ethnic groups in healthy ways; and perhaps even sponsor contests where the person who pitches the latest Disney video the furthest wins a week's visit to the left-wing thinktank of his or her choice.

If my latter suggestion seems a bit much, remember—desperate times call for desperate measures. Having sat through *Aladdin* twice, I'm certain these qualify as desperate times.

notes

1. Edward Said, *Culture and Imperialism* (New York: Alfred A. Knopf, 1993), p. 7.
2. Said, p. 95
3. Said, p. 176.
4. Said, p. 181.
5. Husain Haddawy, *The Arabian Nights* (New York: W.W. Norton, 1990), from the manuscript originally edited by Muhsin Mahdi.

Grey Mourning

In place of Lebanon write
    grey mourning
    land oppressed one thousand times over
    land enchanted one thousand times over.

Miles melt
as grief and dirt
pull us together
after these trauma-filled decades,
two casualties of
relentless marches
by white invaders with
combat boots laced tight
wooden crosses clutched tight
slash and burn
through yellow flesh
brown earth,
only crumpled shadows
left behind.

Now we live with
imperialist militia in the south
northern sections annexed by
a cruel church
staging the same crucifixion
day after day
contrary new languages
grafted onto our tongues.
Lebanon
you're disappearing
as fast as I am.

When I languish
from the latest attack,
overcome with the impossibility
of breathing my way through
one more day,
you feed me,
when anguish sucks me dry
I need olives
from your bloody soil.

Purple bits of sadness
inch across my tongue
right to left,
their salty toughness
revives me,
knife-sharp greeting yanks me
back into battle.

The war external
has plunged me
into war internal
and now
more than ever
I see myself
as your daughter,
another teeming hybrid mass
of chaotic contradictions,
Fairuz behind screams,
smoke bouncing off mirrors,
pride backed up against shame,
all this flanked by
massive scar tissue
and mutilated limbs.

We cling to life
with ruthless determination,
grimly passing through
predictions of imminent demise,
acknowledging grey
as the color
of our sunrise.

Homophobic Workers or Elitist Queers?

*T*hings had not changed, and yet they had. I hopped out at the last stop on the Bloor line westbound and hurriedly followed the "Kiss'n Ride"¹ signs to the cars waiting to pick up passengers. Uncle Joe occupied the driver's seat of the big old red station wagon. All familiar. But four years had passed since I'd spent a Sunday afternoon this way. And now two pairs of feet walked quickly toward the wagon. I was bringing my lover home to meet Uncle Joe and Aunt Chuck, their four kids and partners and grandchildren.

Uncle Joe kissed and hugged Jan and me, then whisked us to the house, where he pulled in the driveway and lay on the horn. Aunt Chuck kissed and hugged us over and over. The cat ran away. I exclaimed over the kitchen; they'd knocked out a wall to make it bigger. "We spend all our time in here anyway," Uncle Joe told Jan. And indeed, my overwhelming memory is of wonderful Sundays spent sitting around that same table in a smaller kitchen and eating and eating and eating and feeling happy. Now, as then, plates crammed with olives, hot peppers, fresh veggies, dips, and bread covered the table. These "snacks" would keep us going until "dinner" began, loose categories since the eating continued all afternoon.

Jan handled herself well, letting Aunt Chuck trip over herself in her haste to bring food and beer. As various cousins arrived on the scene, Jan answered questions from all sides. Where did you grow up? What do you do? What's your cat's name? Where do your brothers live? When did your mother die?

For the brief fifteen minute pause between chowing down on olives and bread ("Eat! Eat! You haven't touched a thing!") and sitting down to the "real" dinner, Jan and I left the group to see Aunt Chuck's flowers at the front of the house. But we couldn't linger because Uncle Joe bellowed at the top of his lungs for my girlfriend: "Jan! Jan! Where are you? Charlotte, I need you to take a picture of me and Jan!"

I recall that day and revel in the feeling of being at home and being loved. Then I consider the enormity and appalling nature of classism in the queer movement.[2] For years I've listened to sweeping, elitist generalizations about the homophobic working-class, to middle- and upper-class queers telling me that the liberal tolerance exhibited by their parents is the best we can expect when bringing our lovers home, to speeches and articles extolling lies about backward "rednecks" who hate queers. Through it all, I tried to hold on to what I know in my bones about working-class people. But what I heard had an impact. For days before our Sunday gathering I felt anxious. Maybe I was wrong in assuming that when I took Jan home to meet these folks, she'd be overwhelmed with love and attention, unquestioningly taken in. Had my years away sugarcoated the reality? Was their love really so strong?

I hadn't sugarcoated anything. I also hadn't put together all the pieces about classism in the queer movement, including the different working-class responses to queers, and the depth, impact, and history of the lie that working-class people are more homophobic than rich people.

A small aside to anyone reading this essay who's not queer. My observations about classism in the queer movement apply equally to other social-change movements, whether environmental, feminist, solidarity, peace. Don't hesitate to analyze your groups with these critiques.

❖　•　❖　•　❖　•　❖

Working-class people's responses to queers vary widely. Some are radically supportive, some are mildly supportive, some don't care much one way or the other, some hate queers viciously and say so to our faces, some stand outside queer bars with baseball bats.

These responses parallel those of the middle and upper classes. Among these groups, some are radically supportive, some mildly supportive, some liberally tolerant, some hate queers viciously and say so. The most homophobic usually don't carry weapons; they've got other ways of maiming and killing us that don't involve anything as "dirty"' as physical assault.[3]

Through friends, I've met radically supportive, upper-middle-class parents and radically supportive working-class parents. Visiting my aunt and uncle solidified my impression of the differences between these groups. Upper-middle-class parents talked openly about queer family members and participated in political work through groups like P-FLAG (Parents and Friends of Lesbians and Gays). Working-class parents didn't join groups, wear buttons, or talk about homophobia to neighbors. Their acceptance of queer family members felt almost casual, as did their integration of queer family members and lovers. They didn't seem the least bit surprised by the presence of queers in the family, and thus didn't make a fuss. I want to explore two issues here: this casual response to the presence of queer family members and the intense love working-class queers get from supportive family members.

First, why aren't working-class people surprised about queers in the family? Maybe working-class people have a better handle on reality. But I'm also intrigued by the word "queer" and possible associations between class identity and sexual identity.

I'm strongly attached to the word "queer," and find it more appropriate than any other for describing my identity. I first read this word as a teenager, where "queer" described girls who refused to obey strict gender codes. This came through in Louisa May Alcott's descriptions of Jo in *Little Women*, and in Lucy Maud Montgomery's portrayal of Valancy in *The Blue Castle*. Today the word queer captures not only my sexual identity, but my class identity as well. It accurately positions me on the margins of the class hierarchy, without any chance of being "normal," that is, middle-class. And the in-your-face power of this word speaks to the pride I experience from my class identity, in strong contrast to the shame I felt growing up.

Figuring out my "queer" working-class identity helped me understand radical acceptance from working-class people. If contented working-class people share a gut feeling of queerness, it's not a total shock when a son comes out as gay. His sexual identity fits with our experiences as "queer" in relation to rich people. My aunt didn't freak out when I said, "I'm a lesbian. I live with my lover." She immediately asked if Jan treats me well, and if she takes care of me. When I reassured her, she said, "That's wonderful." End of discussion.[4]

This lack of surprise over queer family members connects to the kind of love these working-class families feel for each other, and how it impacts the acceptance of queer family members. This love invariably feels deeper than what I've perceived in middle- and upper-middle-class families.

Within working-class families where members love and respect each other (and I'm *not* saying this describes all working-class families), caring for kin is linked to a deep distrust of "the system"—the capitalist system that exploits us and benefits the rich.[5] Our love for each other is tempered and steeled by our exploitation and our need to stick together. We're all we have, so we must stay connected.

Love among working-class people is further differentiated from love among rich people because working-class people can express deep love that springs from honest, unguarded, and clearly-expressed emotions, the kind I've rarely seen in well-off families. Let me clarify this point so I don't reinforce stereotypes. When not vilified, working-class people are often romanticized in particular ways. Don't you recognize us? Warm folk who know how to laugh, cry, and love with abandon, homey folk with hearts of gold who can teach repressed rich people to find happiness in the simple joys of everyday living—walking a dog, sitting on a front porch, enjoying a sunset. Countless books and movies portray these touching little scenarios.

Such romanticized, essentialized versions of working-class life offer rich people a night of cheap entertainment, a few tender tears and crumpled lace handkerchiefs, and a reinforcement of the comforting belief that working-class people aren't scary, angry, threatening, or intelligent. *And* these depictions carry a grain of truth. Working-class people express feelings more than rich people, know how to laugh, cry, and love with abandon, find happiness in everyday life. And not because of anything innate, biological, or essential. These tendencies clearly illustrate the workings of the class system. As working-class people, we haven't been socialized into grim, restrictive sets of manners, social codes, and behaviors. We don't have to act politely and formally, don't have to dole out emotions and feelings carefully and precisely, little bits at a time. Middle- and upper-class people do. The richer they are, the more intense the process. Constraining atmospheres of middle- and upper-class homes reflect this training, which begins early in life.

Working-class people receive little or none of this particular brand of socialization. This doesn't mean we're all emotionally healthy and vibrant, able to express and feel deep, authentic emotion. But there's more possibility for any of this to arise.

❖   ◆   ❖   ◆   ❖   ◆   ❖

While experiencing the pleasure of deep love and radical acceptance from some family members, I've also gone through the anticipated displeasure of vicious queer hatred from other family members, most notably my parents. The night I broke my big news, they said it all. "You're sick. You ought to be locked up in a mental hospital." They expressed disappointment that I was past the age where they could commit me. And clearly my new lifestyle would leave me not only lonely but impoverished. "You'll die penniless in the gutter," my mother informed me.[6] Their disgust wouldn't allow them to even *think* about lesbian sex. Mixed with disgust was pity, followed by anger; they warned me to stay away from my niece, their only grandchild. They wrapped up the whole session with a grand concession: "We won't disown you. But don't ever talk about this again."

Now, homophobia can be tracked to many places—the christian church, fear of sexuality, gendered hierarchies. But what about my parents positioning themselves at the opposite end of the "Queer Response" spectrum from my aunt and uncle? Is the only difference that some of us believe what we're taught? I think not. Class comes into play here.

Working-class homophobes like my parents carry a lot of bitterness which stems in large part from capitalist oppression. They don't accept their lot in life. They want more money, more stuff, and more status. Yet they don't agitate for change; they sit with other like-minded working-class people in resentful anger over the little they've been allowed to acquire.

This bitterness pops up when these people react to "difference,"[7] which they despise and fear in the family, society, themselves. Back to my parents. My father, a dark-skinned Arab, hates being set apart from white norms. He and my mother hate being set apart from middle-class norms, and have no desire to experience "queerness" in relation to those norms. They'd rather make it in the system established by rich people; they'd love to assimilate and be welcomed into the fold. At the same time that they hate rich people, they want to be liked by them and be like them. My parents can't embrace their queerness; they're doing everything possible to escape it. So it makes sense that they let loose with homophobic condemnation when I come out and embrace one particular form of queerness.

I'm convinced one reason for working-class homophobia is this bitterness, this burning desire to fit in with what's "normal," and this factor also helps explain homophobia among the rich. Plenty of wealthy people share my parents' reactions. While some hide their feelings behind a mask of politeness, others express outrageous hatred of queers from a context of bitterness and fear—fear of difference, of not making it, of not living up to the high standards set for them. Alienated and disappointed, they're trying, probably harder than working-class people, to prove their normality and their worth. Queer children interfere with this plan.

Then there's another problem. If they admit sexual difference is not only possible but acceptable, they may have to perceive other differences as acceptable. Then what happens to their belief in superior status?

❖　•　❖　•　❖　•　❖

Similarities come to the foreground when explaining why homophobia exists in different classes, but only one class is classified outright as the most homophobic. Working-class/working-poor people claim the dubious honor of being dubbed more homophobic (and more racist, and more sexist) than rich people. This holds true in mainstream society, queer organizations, and other progressive movements.

Middle-class and upper-middle-class queers respond with boring predictability when I claim my working-class identity. They assume I can't be out, either in my family or my working-class neighborhood, because of unchecked and assaultive homophobia rampant in these arenas. When I contradict them, they either look at me with awe for my bravery or ask, in hushed tones, just how badly everything went. Although I enjoy giving these people an elaborate, lengthy recital of my aunt and uncle's treatment of Jan and me, underneath I'm angry and concerned. Why is this idea so prevalent? How did it get started? Who benefits?

With the passage of time and greater "successes," the capitalist system has sharpened its ability to spread misinformation and foster class and race divisions. Lies about backward, unenlightened poor people have been around forever and a day. This ensures our status as Other and our availability for drudge work at shit wages.

The advent of the Black civil rights movement reinforced this idea. While articulate, radical working-class activists from all racial/ethnic groups participated in this movement, they're not the ones well-remembered four decades later. Americans do remember the white, southern, working-class men and women who spoke against desegregation, sneered at "niggers," and didn't mince words about their hatred. Why do we remember? Because the media highlighted them, over and over and over again. The media provided ample TV time, airplay, and newspaper photos.

These racist interviewees spoke clearly and to the point, in true working-class fashion. They had no reason to hide their thoughts and feelings, nothing to gain from lying. Nor had they spent years honing verbal skills that would allow them to cover up their real feelings and present a reasonable, caring, and polite facade to the world.

Meanwhile, back at the ranch, the media simply ignored white people with the power to devise, reinforce, and carry out brutally racist practices. After all, ownership has its privileges! The few times camera lights shone toward rich white people, they manipulated language, smiled, wore nice clothes, and said their university or state or business *wanted* equality; they just hoped it would happen the right way.

The ruling class emerged from this battle looking a whole lot better than working-class white people. Through subsequent decades, rich people have continued to bask in the glow of the winners' circle lights, as progressive middle-class people consistently cast working-class people unfavorably. Consider environmental movements of the 1970s and 1980s. I vividly remember activists targeting Newfoundland fishermen who clubbed baby seals to death. An ardent supporter of animal liberation and a long-time vegetarian, I hated what happened to the seals. Just as much as I hated what happened to the fishermen. Having visited Newfoundland and seen the poverty, I had no quarrel with the fishermen. Why didn't activists challenge the people who had the power to change the situation?[8]

This problematic politic reinforced a viewpoint traditionally fostered by the ruling class—that of stupid, unenlightened, backward workers. Now middle-class activists reinforced and strengthened this belief. In the peace movement, activists denounced workers for taking jobs at munitions plants. In the environmental movement, activists denounced selfish loggers for not caring about the spotted owl. I rarely heard owners criticized and called to account.

These profound and sad examples resulted from community organizing without an integrated analysis of oppression, in particular without a class analysis. Through the 1960s, 1970s, and 1980s, incomplete analyses and problematic actions by progressive, middle-class activists supported the ruling class and offered new fodder in the war against working-class and working-poor people. The media, owned by the ruling class, happily took notes about selfish loggers and offered prominent air time. Corporate owners sat complacently behind the scenes. As usual. Although I have no direct contact with these people, I assume they appreciated the classist and anti-environmental ideas verbalized time and again over the airwaves. I assume they appreciated reinforcement of the image of the backward, expendable, stupid laborer.

So many benefits to the ruling class! First, class divisions are heightened and reinforced. Second, focus is redirected away from the harmful, retrograde, and oppressive ideas of the ruling class and toward workers. Third, organizers act as unthinking accomplices for the ruling class. Fourth, the grim reality of who has power to keep homophobia, racism, and classism securely in place is obscured, as it has been for a long time.

In examining this point, I'm not saying working-class people are empty mouthpieces who can't think for ourselves; we're quite capable of devising our own homophobic ideas. I do want to articulate the difference between our homophobia and the homophobia of the rich. Truck drivers and garbage men don't determine social policies. We don't make laws and decide what's acceptable and what's not. Wealthy people hold that power. They don't wait for us outside queer bars to beat us up; that's a working-class response for sure. But wealthy people do occupy judges' benches and presidents' offices and corporate boardrooms, and devise policies that ensure our children will be stolen, our relationships outlawed, our jobs taken, our partners denied health insurance. The queer movement must clearly name the powerful homophobes and strategize how to go after them.

❖　◆　❖　◆　❖　◆　❖

I'm saddened, but not surprised, that the queer movement hasn't steered clear of this pitfall of middle-class progressive movements. Every step of the way it has swallowed the lie hook, line, and sinker, and belief about the homophobic working-class sits firmly ensconced in political action and theory. A right-wing, homophobic response emerges as the only possible and authentic working-class response to queerness, a portrayal with several harmful ramifications. First, angry working-class and working-poor queers. And rightfully so. Classism permeates every level of the queer movement. How much can a social-change movement achieve when wrought with classist arrogance?

Second, for the past decades the queer movement has lost the chance to build ties and links with a natural ally—working-class and working-poor people. When I first came out, I couldn't understand why queer activists didn't attend union meetings and join picket lines. What better place to build bridges and engage in solidarity work? Then I realized classism prevents queer activists, leaders, and organizers from even considering the idea.

Third, poor people and queers are linked in critical ways. Extensive crossover exists between these groups. Lots of queers are firmly situated among working-class and working-poor communities, and 10 percent of this group outnumbers 10 percent from the middle- and upper-classes. Don't disguise reality by configuring us as the minority.[9] Also, queers and poor people share common agendas. Central concerns of working-class/working-poor people have recently been taken on by AIDS activists—nationalized health care and protection from unemployment. Another common struggle stems from restrictive definitions of the "family" that not only cast queers as sick and other, but also attach that label to single mothers, common-law heterosexual partners, extended families, and various other conglomerations of people that end up living together under working-class roofs.

However, to date the queer movement has focused on alliance-building with rich people. No one has explicitly drafted this strategy; it happens because middle- and upper-class leadership steers toward people and institutions they know. With current assimilationist attitudes, it's even worse. When I flew to D.C. for the 1993 Queer March on Washington, I thought I would throw up if I heard one more TV interview with an earnest, middle-class queer explaining, "We're just like everyone else. This march will prove that." For the phrase "everyone else," read middle-class, white, monogamous, heterosexual couple. Don't read poor Chicana single mom.

Over the years I've been told, explicitly and implicitly, that liberal tolerance offered by rich people is the best queers can hope for. This needs analyzing, since it's a reaction that doesn't cut across class lines—that is, liberal tolerance only shows up in certain places. I'm happy to report I've never spotted the veneer of polite acceptance in working-class company, although it's rampant among the rich. Everyone's smiling, perhaps with a tinge of artificiality, and no one says anything nasty, but it's a far cry from being loved, welcomed, or integrated as a matter of course. It means I'm *tolerated*, that is, allowed to sit in the same room as people who know they rank above me. Is this really the best we can hope for? I refuse to accept that. While sitting in proper living rooms, I'm sizzling. I refuse to settle for condescending, patronizing tolerance from people who, underneath bland smiles and small talk, think much the same as my parents.

Liberal tolerance angers and irritates me, and I'm thankful it's not part of any working-class reality I've ever encountered. I can't deal with uptight rich folks who won't say shit when they step in it, who won't say queer when we fill up their living rooms. In the same way that working-class African Americans who grew up in the South and now live in the North have told me they prefer the more overt racism of the South, I deal better with working-class homophobes than with middle- or upper-class patronizingly tolerant homophobes. With the working-class person, I know where I stand, when to run, and when to talk. Someone who says to my face, "You're sick," might listen while I explain why I'm not. I can't argue with a person who *thinks* I'm sick and politely offers me tea, but I can engage with an honest factory worker. Change is never guaranteed, but in some cases it happens when we talk one on one about our sexuality. I predict it will happen even more if/when our actions as a movement prove we understand and care about the same bread-and-butter issues.

❖　•　❖　•　❖　•　❖

Working-class and working-poor queers who found each other in urban centers in the 1950s and 1960s ran the gamut from kiki to drag kings and queens to butch-femme couples to bull dykes. They toughed it out on the streets and did the best they could to resist extreme brutality and social scorn. But these folks weren't accorded leadership roles, let alone respect, in the larger movements for queer liberation that formed in the 1970s and 1980s. Sometimes they couldn't get in the door. When they managed to, they didn't have a powerful role in shaping the movement and neither did younger working-class queers. Instead, middle-class and upper-middle-class queers shaped the strategies and actions of the past three decades. I'm disturbed by the push for alliance with the corporate board room and not the union hall, by the invisibility of working-class queers, by a refusal to take class seriously.

I want the same things from the queer movement that I want from other social-change movements: a clear agenda, an inclusive definition of the group in question, an integrated analysis of all oppressions, a focus on coalition building.

First, I want the queer movement to articulate a clear agenda of ending heterosexist/homophobic oppression, of integrating and welcoming all queers into the movement, of supporting liberation movements for disabled people/people of color/working-class and working-poor people/women. I want non-disabled queers at disability rights rallies stating support and a willingness to go to bat. I want non-union-member queers on picket lines. I wait for the day when we reap the benefits of solidarity work, and straight folks in wheelchairs and heterosexual welfare mothers speak at our demos and advocate on our behalf.

Second, I want a queer movement with a clear policy defining queer people and welcoming anyone who self-identifies as queer. While this seems so basic it's not worth mentioning, in reality it's critically important because so many queers have been left out of the movement's stated and unstated definitions. Bisexuals and transgender/transsexual people experience routine exclusion, as do queers of color, queers in wheelchairs, working-poor/working-class queers.[10] The queer movement needs to clearly articulate who we are, state that anyone who self-identifies as queer is welcome, and then—here's the tough part—not freak out when the drag queens and kings, the trannies, and the high femmes arrive in full force. Or in full drag, which may be even scarier.

Third, the queer movement needs an integrated analysis of all oppressions. For queers to focus only on homophobia and heterosexism, without understanding racism, classism, imperialism, sexism, and ableism, is morally wrong and politically dangerous. This type of shallow analysis ignores the presence of queers living with more than one oppression, indirectly supports other oppressions through complicit silence, situates our struggle outside of other liberation movements, feeds isolation, and cuts us off from the power of connecting with others in struggle.

Fourth, while I always support coalition building, it's especially important during this particular time, when overt right-wing individuals and groups continue to gain political power. Coalition building displays an understanding of the connected strands of all oppressions, and firmly situates queers within the context of the struggle for social justice. It affirms the identity of queers who belong to more than one oppressed group, and allows us to do what we need to do—for example, connect our struggle to end racism with our struggle to end heterosexism. And coalition building, which directly challenges divide-and-conquer strategies, presents a fiercer challenge to the powers that be than a single-issue campaign ever could.

❖ ◆ ❖ ◆ ❖ ◆ ❖

The night after that sunlit day at Aunt Chuck and Uncle Joe's, Jan and I hung out with various cousins. Sitting in a room thick with smoke from cigarettes and joints, I tried to explain what my aunt and uncle's response meant, what it felt like to have my partner so accepted and welcomed and pulled tight into the heart of this family I love.

My cousins pursed their lips and frowned. They didn't understand me, and kept saying: "Of course that happened. Why wouldn't it? This is your family. We care about you."

I gave up trying to explain, because I understood. *What else would we do?* I wondered how many anti-homophobia workshops rich people would have to attend before understanding, in their bones, the utter truth and simplicity and casualness of that understanding: *what else would we do?*

notes

1. This is an area at certain Toronto subway stops where people in cars can park and wait for subway riders.
2. I use the term "queer movement" as a shorthand in this piece to describe the various queer political organizations in the United States at this point in time. I know there are different movements and communities, and in some ways it's inappropriate to lump them together, but in other ways it's not. I also know that while working-poor and working-class queers are active in these organizations, the structure and leadership is middle and upper-middle class. Classism is apparently a low priority in these groups at this time.
3. Privileged young men on college campuses offer an exception to prove that rule.
4. It's difficult to say how Arab culture fits into my aunt's response. While openness and tolerance have always been important values in the Arab world, this hasn't always crossed over into the responses of Arab-Canadians and Arab Americans whose family members come out as queer. I plan to explore this issue in later essays.
5. When I use the word "rich" in this essay, I'm using it in the way most working-class people I know use it—anyone middle-class and up is rich, anyone working-class and down is poor. In some ways these two categories are not subtle enough for all the nuances around class; one thing they do is hide my privilege of being working-class but not working-poor. On the other hand, I find "rich" and "poor" powerful, provocative, and appropriate categories. Middle-class people, who could choose to realize they are also being duped by rich people and decide they would be better off aligning themselves with working-class and working-poor people, continually align themselves with the rich. Thus, including the middle-class people in the "rich" group is appropriate. So to the middle-class queers reading this— when I use the word rich, I mean you.
6. This comment does make sense, in terms of my mother's gut knowledge of how class and gender oppression work together. One of the hardest

things I had to face when I came out was knowing that when I left my middle-class husband, I'd be poor, and would probably stay that way the rest of my life.

7. I'm putting this problematic word in quotation marks to signify my concern. Even using this word can reinforce the social belief that carefully fostered race, class, and gender divisions are natural.

8. Thanks to Jan Binder for helping me articulate this point.

9. Privileged groups love to insist they're the majority, especially around race. Although as people of color, we're clearly the majority in terms of world population, the term "minority group" is continually used to describe us. Does this semantic distortion allow oppressors to feel less frightened about hordes of poor, dark people that massively outnumber them and have reason to despise them?

10. This is no different from people of color who don't know what to do with halfbreeds and feminists who don't know what to do with members of transgender communities.

Lines

Chase latitude and longitude,
stop when one forefinger
finds the eastern bit
of Europe and the other
lights on Asia's western edge,
ponder this peasant lineage
and our skewed relationships
to straight geometric elements
generated by the harsh realities
of beginnings, endings, middles
through (un)stable points of reference.
Now the taut thread knots me
into the center of this tangled mass.

Lives jangled by lines;
measure scraps of land with string,
plow straight grooves,
measure water, measure grain
with scrupulous care.
Always a furrow between the eyebrows
leading directly to unlined pockets,
shadow this unequal triangle
again and again
until hard creases at the corners
of stubborn mouths
abruptly dissect it.

Hunger drops unceremoniously
in the straightest of lines,
plunging directly from bare table
to mouth to stomach to intestine
to food-filled dreams
and morning's despair.

Our names can be unearthed
in history books
but only by the most diligent;
sift letters
decipher blank space
between even rows
until buried codes and symbols
scratched out by our broken pencils
bump up against searching fingers.

Through this last century
we've proceeded diligently
across the planet,
treading well-worn paths.
From small pocket of dirt
to dark corner in boat
to earth marked by
someone else's beaded signposts,
then lurch from job to job
until working the line secures us.

My present line
follows family tradition —
magic
my grandparents' trick
pull survival from thin air
I cling to the same top-hat
practice with scarves, rabbits, coins
determined to catch
pieces of these ancestors
before they reach

the point of no return,
force this apparition of a pen
to reinstate them
on a lined page.

$\mathcal{P}ermissions$

rateful acknowledgments to the following individuals and publishers, who allowed us to include these works in this collection:

"Frightening Bedfellows: Pop Culture and Imperialism," originally appeared under the title "Disney's Dominion" in *Colors* magazine, Minneapolis, Minnesota, January-February 1995.

"Moving from Cultural Appropriation to Ethical Cultural Connections" originally appeared in *Colors* magazine, Minneapolis, Minnesota, November-December 1993.

"Stupidity 'Deconstructed'" was written for the forthcoming book *Social Justice, Feminism, and the Politics of Location*. Many thanks to the Center for Advanced Feminist Studies editorial committee at University of Minnesota for allowing it to be printed here.

"Writing as Love, Writing as Resistance" originally appeared under the title "My World Split Open" in *Colors* magazine, Minneapolis, Minnesota, September-October 1994.

Index

A

ableism, 73-76
    allies with survivors of, 79
abortion, 65-66
abuse. *See also* child abuse, child
    sexual abuse, rape, *and* ritual
    abuse
    emotional, 70
    physical, 65-66, 70
academia, and class, 39-57
activism, 13, 18, 20, 83, 85-87,
    136-137, 150, 152
    civil disobedience, 26
    feminist, 71-72, 84-85, 103-104
African continent, 118, 131
Aladdin, 129-137
Alcott, Louisa May, 145
algebra, 13
Algeria, 131
All In the Family, 48
alliances
    across cultural lines, 120, 123,
        124, 127
    queer, across class lines, 152-
        153
    with child abuse survivors, 70
    with disabled activists, 79
Allison, Dorothy, 3
alphabet, 13
American continent, 118, 131
American Sign Language, 87

ancestors, 14, 160
animal liberation, 150
anti-depressant, 76
Antigua, 130-131
Arab, 6, 9-11, 13, 14, 47, 64, 116,
    118, 122, 126, 131-132, 148
    culture, 13, 18-20, 24-25, 115-
        119, 121, 123-127, 135,
        136
    immigrants, 25, 30, 31
    nationalism, 132
    positive images of, 10-11, 13
    racism against, 9-10, 77-78,
        115, 119, 123, 129, 132-
        134
    world, 13, 129, 133
Arabian Nights, The, 136
Aristotle, 43
art, 17-26
    classification of, 19
    criticism, 21, 97, 100-101, 106
    ethnic, 19-20
    traditional, 19-20
Asia, 159
Asian continent, 118, 131
assimilation, 56, 115, 122
Aunt Rose, 17-26
Austen, Jane, 130-131

B

barn raisings, 5
battered women, 71, 75

THINKING CLASS

debke, 17, 20, 23-24, 25
  Indonesian, 19
  two-stepping, 22-23
debke. *See* dance
DeMent, Iris, 98, 99, 100, 105
depression, 71
derbeke. *See* drums/drumming
difference, 148-149
dogs, 5, 7, 59-60
doll-making, 19
drag queens and kings, 55, 154,
  155. *See also* queer
drums/drumming, 115-127
  congas, 116
  derbeke, 115-120, 123-127
Du Bois, W. E. B., 46
Dworkin, Andrea, 87

E

educational system, 33-37, 63-67,
  109-112
Elliott, 57, 106, 107
Episcopal Divinity School, 40
ethical cultural connections, 115-
  127
ethnic studies, 54
Europe, 159
exoticization of Asian women, 77

F

factory workers, 29, 34, 37, 40, 47,
  48, 94
Fairhart, Jim, 3
Fairuz, 140
Fancy, 103
Farrar, Sally Ann, 3
fascism, 136
FBI (Federal Bureau of Investiga-
  tion), 87
Feinberg, Leslie, 3
France, 131
Freud, Sigmund, 70

G

garbage men, 55, 151
gay activism. *See* queer politics
gender, 63-67, 72
general motors, 34, 41, 45, 48, 67,
  112
genocide, 120, 125
Gentry, Bobbie, 103
Georgia On My Mind, 95
Gill, Vince, 105
government, 73, 129, 132, 133
graduate school, 42-43
grandparents, 6, 42, 49, 160
Gulf War, 10, 116, 133

H

Haddawy, Husain, 136
halfbreed, 59-60, 64, 157
health care, national, 86, 151, 152
history
  of universities, 47
  of theory, 40
  textbooks, 160
Hmong embroidery, 19
homophobia, 145, 147-149
Honeymooners, The, 48
housecleaning, 53, 54, 55, 93
Huebner, Marjorie, 3, 26
humor, 25, 39, 51, 97
hunger, 160
hybrid, 140

I

I Got It Honest, 93
I Love Lucy, 48
I Wanna Hold Your Hand, 112
identity
  class, 20, 24-25, 52-54, 145-
    146, 149
  race, 54, 64, 77, 119-120
  rural, 95-96, 105
  sexual, 145-146
I'm So Lonesome I Could Cry, 94

166

smoking, 17, 20, 33, 35, 42, 44, 56, 64, 155
Socrates, 43
South (southern U.S.), 43, 94-95, 105, 149, 153
speech, 12
spin-the-bottle, 33, 35
spotted owl, 150
Stonewall riots, 55
story-telling, 13, 25, 136
stupidity, 9, 39-57, 63, 94
street person, 12
suicide, 71
Suzuki, Linda, 3

T

terror, 12, 14, 69, 71
theory, 40, 47, 69-87
    feminist, 71, 74
therapy, 70, 71
Tippin, Aaron, 93, 105, 106
tongues, 10, 29, 41, 43, 89-91, 139
Toronto, 97, 156
Toronto, University of, 40, 42
torture, 70, 87
transgender/transsexual people, 155, 157. *See also* queer
truck drivers, 9, 94, 151
truth, 6, 12, 13, 14

U

UAW (United Auto Workers), 34

union, 34, 110, 111, 152
United States of America, 133, 156
university. *See* academia
upward mobility, 44-45, 54

V

violence, horizontal, 123

W

waitresses, 94
Walt Disney, 129, 132-137
Washington, D.C., 116
Western thought, 6, 50, 100-101
Williams, Hank, 94, 106
Women's Studies, 54
Workin Man's Ph.D., 105
working-class
    culture, 7, 17-26, 93-107
    positive images of, 13
    stereotypes of, 48-49, 134, 149-151
    studies, 55
writing, 5-7, 9-14
writing system, 13

Y

Yoakam, Dwight, 101

Z

Zemsky, Beth, 3

A NOTE TO OUR READERS

South End Press is a nonprofit, collectively run book publisher with over 180 titles in print. Since our founding in 1977, we have tried to meet the needs of readers who are exploring, or are already committed to, the politics of radical social change.

Our goal is to publish books that encourage critical thinking and constructive action on the key political, cultural, social, economic, and ecological issues shaping life in the United States and in the world. In this way, we hope to give expression to a wide diversity of democratic social movements and to provide an alternative to the products of corporate publishing.

Through the Institute for Social and Cultural Change, South End Press works with other political media projects—Z Magazine; Speak Out!, a speakers' bureau; Alternative Radio; and the Publishers' Support Project—to expand access to information and critical analysis.

For a free catalog, please write to South End Press, 7 Brookline St, #1, Cambridge, MA 02139; call 1-800-533-8478; or visit our website at http://www.lbbs.org.

Related Titles of Interest

Glass Ceilings and Bottomless Pits
Women's Work, Women's Poverty
by Randy Albelda and Chris Tilley
$18.00 paper; $40.00 cloth

Regulating the Lives of Women
Social Welfare Policy from Colonial Times to the Present
(Revised edition, 1996)
by Mimi Abramovitz
$22.00 paper; $40.00 cloth

Chaos or Community?
Seeking Solutions, Not Scapegoats, to Bad Economics
by Holly Sklar
$15.00 paper; $35.00 cloth

Race, Gender, and Work
A Multi-cultural Economic History of Women in the United States
(Revised edition, 1996)
by Teresa Amott and Julie Matthaei
$21.00 paper; $40.00 cloth

Poverty in the American Dream
Women and Children First
by Karin Stallard, Barbara Ehrenreich, and Holly Sklar
$6.00 paper

Women in the Global Factory
by Annette Fuentes and Barbara Ehrenreich
$6.00 paper

Mink Coats Don't Trickle Down
The Economic Attack on Women & People of Color
by Randy Albelda, Elaine McCrate, Edwin Melendez, June Lapidus,
and The Center for Popular Economics
$5.00 paper

Black Liberation in Conservative America
by Manning Marable
$16.00 paper; $40.00 cloth

Another America
The Politics of Race and Blame
by Kofi Buenor Hadjor
$15.00 paper; $40.00 cloth

A True Story of a Drunken Mother
by Nancy Lee Hall
$8.00 paper; $25.00 cloth

A True Story of a Single Mother
by Nancy Lee Hall
$8.00 paper

Sisterhood and Solidarity
Feminism and Labor in Modern Times
by Diane Balser
$10.00 paper; $35.00 cloth

Power on the Job
The Legal Rights of Working People
by Michael Yates
$16.00 paper; $30.00 cloth

Triumph of the Market
Essays on Economics, Politics and the Media
by Edward S. Herman
$16.00 paper; $40.00 cloth

When ordering, please include $3.50 postage and handling for the first book and 50 cents
for each additional book. To order by credit card, call 1-800-533-8478.

About the Author

Joanna Kadi is a writer, poet, editor, and musician. In addition to having had numerous essays and short stories published, she is the editor of *Food for our Grandmothers: Writings by Arab-American and Arab-Canadian Feminists*, also published by South End Press. Kadi has worked as a grassroots community organizer on a diverse range of issues, including Palestinian self-determination and ending violence against women. She teaches classes in critical thinking for the Center for Arts Criticism (Minneapolis) and the GLBT Programs Office at the University of Minnesota.

About South End Press

South End Press is a nonprofit, collectively run book publisher with more than 200 titles in print. Since our founding in 1977, we have tried to meet the needs of readers who are exploring, or are already committed to, the politics of radical social change. Our goal is to publish books that encourage critical thinking and constructive action on the key political, cultural, social, economic, and ecological issues shaping life in the United States and in the world. In this way, we hope to give expression to a wide diversity of democratic social movements and to provide an alternative to the products of corporate publishing.

Through the Institute for Social and Cultural Change, South End Press works with other political media projects—Alternative Radio; Speakout, a speakers' bureau; and *Z Magazine*—to expand access to information and critical analysis.

To order books, please send a check or money order to: South End Press, 7 Brookline Street, #1, Cambridge, MA 02139-4146. To order by credit card, call 1-800-533-8478. Please include $3.50 for postage and handling for the first book and 50 cents for each additional book.

Write or e-mail southend@southendpress.org for a free catalog, or visit our web site at www.southendpress.org.